Library of Shakespearean Biography and Criticism

I. PRIMARY REFERENCE WORKS ON SHAKESPEARE

II. CRITICISM AND INTERPRETATION
    A. Textual Treatises, Commentaries
    B. Treatment of Special Subjects
    C. Dramatic and Literary Art in Shakespeare

III. SHAKESPEARE AND HIS TIME
    A. General Treatises. Biography
    B. The Age of Shakespeare
    C. Authorship

Library of Shakespearean Biography and Criticism

Series II, Part A

HAMLET THROUGH THE AGES

HAMLET FROM A STAGE BOX, 1857

An early photo-montage for a stereoscope slide. The playbill is for a performance at Drury Lane on 16 April, 1857, with Charles Dillon as Hamlet and Mrs. Weston as Gertrude.

𝕷ibrary of 𝕾hakespearean 𝕭iography and 𝕮riticism

Hamlet
through the ages

*A
Pictorial Record
from 1709
compiled by*

RAYMOND MANDER & JOE MITCHENSON

Edited with an Introduction by
HERBERT MARSHALL

Second Edition

BOOKS FOR LIBRARIES PRESS
FREEPORT, NEW YORK

First published in 1952 by Rockliff Books
Copyright © by Raymond Mander and Joe Mitchenson

Revised edition 1955
Copyright © by Raymond Mander and Joe Mitchenson

Reprinted 1971 by arrangement with
Raymond Mander and Joe Mitchenson, and their literary
agent, London Management and Representation, Ltd.

INTERNATIONAL STANDARD BOOK NUMBER:
0-8369-5677-X

LIBRARY OF CONGRESS CATALOG CARD NUMBER:
70-148888

PRINTED IN THE UNITED STATES OF AMERICA

TO ALL THOSE ACTORS WHO IN THE PAST HAVE
PLAYED HAMLET AND TO THOSE WHO IN THE FUTURE
WILL FOLLOW IN THEIR TRADITION—THIS
BOOK IS DEDICATED

ACKNOWLEDGMENTS

THE pictures are drawn mostly from our own collection, but we wish to thank all those people who have been so helpful with material and information. Among those who have contributed we would like to record our sincere gratitude to the late Mrs. Gabrielle Enthoven, O.B.E., and Mr. George Nash of the Enthoven Collection at the Victoria and Albert Museum. Mr. M. W. Stone, for allowing us to reproduce sheets from his magnificent collection of the Juvenile Drama. The Committee of the Garrick Club for permission to reproduce pictures in their collection. Mr. George Speaight of Messrs. Benjamin Pollock, Ltd., for allowing the Viennese Model Theatre to be photographed. Mr. John Vickers for making the copy of an old photograph for the Frontispiece. Dr. Böhm for German and Austrian photographs which he had taken. Dr. Carl Niessen and Messrs. Kohlhammer of Stuttgart, for permission to reproduce (No. 34), from their book: *Shakespeare and the German Theatre*, by E. L. Stahl. Mr. Alec Clunes and the Arts Theatre Club for photographs of their production. The J. Arthur Rank Organization and Sir Laurence Olivier for the use of film stills. Miss Norah Traylan of the British Film Institute for her help. Miss Muriel Martin-Harvey for the loan of photographs. Mr. Herbert Steiniger of Munich, who, while on a visit to London, checked the German notes and gave valuable assistance. The Society for Cultural Relations with the U.S.S.R. and similar organizations abroad for the loan of photographs. Mr. Tyrone Guthrie for photographs and information of his Elsinore *Hamlet*. Mr. J. Grant Anderson for a photograph of the Indian National Theatre Company. The Librarian of the Memorial Theatre Library, Stratford-upon-Avon, for information and permission to use photographs taken by Messrs. Daniels and Holte. The Librarian of the Vic-Wells Association, for information. The Bristol Old Vic for permission to use photographs taken by Mr. Desmond Tripp (Nos. 100 and 135). The National Portrait Gallery, the British Museum, the Victoria and Albert Museum, for photographs. Dr. Van Lennep and his assistants of the Harvard College Theatre Collection, Mr. George Freedley of the New York Public Library Theatre Collection, and John Brünnick of the National Open-air Stage, Copenhagen, for information.

For modern photographs we thank: Cyril Arapoff (Nos. 24 and 80), Cecil Beaton (Nos. 168 and 222), British Broadcasting Corporation (Nos. 220 and 249), Howard Coster (No. 56), the *Daily Mirror* (Nos. 43, 107, 170, 186, 231 and 232), J. W. Debenham (No. 127), Yvonne Gregory (No. 190), International News Photos, New York (No. 133), Lenare (Nos. 113, 114, 161 and 236), The London News Agency (No. 55), Angus McBean (Nos. 127, 136 and 224), Edward Mandinian (Nos. 25, 84, 86, 165 and 221), Odhams Photo Library (Nos. 19, 57, 61, 81, 83, 85, 217, 218 and 244), Bertram Park (Nos. 18, 54, 125, 140, 214 and 238), *Picture Post* Library (No. 201), Ramsay and Muspratt (Nos. 50 and 129), Houston Rogers (No. 248), Sasha (Nos. 17, 93, 115 and 189), the *Scotsman* (No. 52), Tunbridge (No. 250), John Vickers (No. 247).

ACKNOWLEDGMENTS

We would like to put on record our thanks for the untiring work of Miss Patricia Hill in transcribing notes and drafting the index, and also to Miss Frances Fleetwood for similar work. To anyone we have inadvertently omitted we offer our apologies and thanks.

RAYMOND MANDER
and
JOE MITCHENSON

PREFACE TO THE SECOND EDITION

SINCE this book was first published in October 1952 there have been a number of productions of *Hamlet* in various parts of the world, and we have included notes of some of the most interesting and important, which range from the Old Vic in London and Elsinore, a modern-dress production in repertory, to productions in Germany and Italy. In Scandinavia alone there were six different productions of the play to be seen between July 1953 and June 1954. (This included the Old Vic production at Elsinore.) London also saw a fine straightforward production at the Embassy Theatre in 1953 with Laurence Payne as Hamlet. In America, where this book was published in 1953, there have been productions in a reconstruction of an Elizabethan Playhouse at Oregon (1954), among others of less note.

We have revised several notes, to bring the book into line with new research, and made corrections where necessary. We received reviews for this book from as far afield as Australia, Brazil, Greece and India, as well as the nearer Scandinavian countries and Holland, testifying to the universal appeal of *Hamlet*.

To those who have written to us with suggestions and helped us to keep this book up to date, we tender our sincere thanks. We also wish to thank Her Majesty the Queen for permission to reproduce for the first time the watercolour in the Library at Windsor Castle of the Charles Kean Command Performance, 1849. This has so far only been seen in its engraved form; to Sir Ashley and Lady Clarke for their help in tracing pictures of the Italian production, here reproduced by courtesy of the *Enciclopedia dello Spettacolo*; Mr. Geoffrey Edwards, for his kind response to our request for photographs and data on his modern-dress production at Bromley; Mr. Raymond Mould, for keeping us up to date with Scandinavia; Mr. M. W. Stone for his valuable research into the history of the Juvenile Drama sheets; the Trustees of the National Theatre, for allowing us to reproduce the painting No. 101a, from the W. Somerset Maugham Collection; and to the following photographers:—
No. 254, Keystone Press Agency; 255, Angus McBean; 183a, Victoria & Albert Museum, Enthoven Collection.

RAYMOND MANDER
and
JOE MITCHENSON
February, 1955.

CONTENTS

	PAGE
Acknowledgments	viii
Introduction	xi
Act I, Scene 1 : Elsinore, a Platform before the Castle	1
Scene 2 : A Room of State in the Castle	9
Scene 3 : A Room in Polonius's House	17
Scenes 4 and 5 : The Platform, and another part of the Platform	22
Act II, Scene 1 : A Room in Polonius's House	45
Scene 2 : A Room in the Castle	45
Act III, Scene 1 : A Room in the Castle	60
Scene 2 : A Hall in the Castle	66
Scene 3 : A Room in the Castle (The King's Closet)	88
Scene 4 : The Queen's Closet	92
Act IV, Scene 1 : A Room in the Castle	104
Scene 2 : Another Room in the Castle	106
Scene 3 : Another Room in the Castle	106
Scene 4 : A Plain in Denmark	108
Scene 5 : A Room in the Castle	111
Scene 6 : Another Room in the Castle	119
Scene 7 : Another Room in the Castle	119
Act V, Scene 1 : A Churchyard	120
Scene 2 : A Hall in the Castle	136
Index	154
Actors as Hamlet	154
Other Actors	154
Producers	156
Designers	156
Countries, Towns and Theatres	157
Miscellaneous	158

Endpapers

Title page, First Quarto, 1603
Title page, First Folio, 1623
Playbill, Drury Lane Theatre—Hamlet : David Garrick, 1756
Playbill, Princess's Theatre—Hamlet : Charles Kean, 1850

INTRODUCTION

THE art of the theatre is an ephemeral art. Though, alas, no art is eternal! Even the basalt statues of the Pharaohs—hardest of all rock—even these shall pass away into the desert dust. Nevertheless, even in a relative sense the ephemeral life of theatre art—apart from its literary aspect—is heartbreakingly short.

What would we not give to know really how Duse acted, or Irving produced or how Shakespeare's company played at the Globe? How did an Antoine production compare with Molière? Or the Saxe-Meiningen with Reinhardt or Piscator? How did Gordon Craig's Shakespeare production compare with Granville-Barker's? Alas, apart from a few photographs, some sketches and engravings, a painting or two, some haphazard notes of the producer or designer, some reviews in the Press, and a morass of memoirs, hardly anything else remains from which to reconstruct the whole production. A prehistoric monster can be reconstructed from a single fossil, and a scientist has a fairly exact idea of its habits and its life, even though it may have been extinct for thousands of years, but a theatre production cannot similarly be so exactly reconstructed from its producer's notes or its artist's sketches or a diarist's memoirs even after five years! It is too complex and dynamic a phenomenon to be re-conceived from one of its parts.

Nevertheless, nowadays there is a technical form, to which only this age could have given birth, the sound-colour-cinema which could record at least the high spots of our theatre's greatness. That is the most advanced form possible for recording, until the sound-colour-stereoscopic-cinema is available. Yet, not to mention this most advanced form, even the most primitive are not consistently used to record our passing theatre history! Already Laurence Olivier's Oedipus Rex and Mr. Puff are a memory; a few photographs, some reviews, and an essay or so—no more. And that was on the boards, a living thing, a few years ago! Ralph Richardson's Falstaff or Uncle Vanya are gone with the wind, and hardly an archive remains.

This is not only a sad thing; it is a shameful thing. Even if our National Theatre cannot afford to make a cinematographic record of some of its best work, at least it should do all else that remains and make use of the cheaper and simpler forms of documentation. But even when this was proposed by the writer, its importance was not understood. During the Old Vic's peak period, with Laurence Olivier, Ralph Richardson, Michel Saint-Denis and John Burrell, I offered to compile and publish a complete Production Record using the existing prompt copies; the notes of the producer; sketches and final drawings of the designer; material from the actors and participants; selected reproductions of every scene design; action photographs of the high spots of every scene, together with every critical review worthy of the name and special articles from the leading protagonists. But after a twelve months' procrastination the Old Vic turned it down! Since then, there have been some photographic albums and monographs of one kind or another, but not the thorough many-sided compilations I proposed.

And the incredible paucity and careless disregard of theatre archives have only been brought home to us while working on this present publication. But before going into this in more detail, I will first explain the origin of the idea of this book.

As a theatre producer, preparing a production, I am of the school that studies everything that has any relationship to the play and the subject-matter. In studying the lives of many creative personalities, it has become clear that all of them have absorbed, in one way or another, the creative work of their predecessors and even of their contemporaries. In their need for creative nutriment they have spurned nothing, have had no false pride or modesty in learning and imbibing others' works, nor any pseudo-romantic conception that artistic somethings come from non-artistic nothings.

There are producers and actors who have said: "I'm not going to see so-and-so's interpretation of *Hamlet* in case I get influenced!" Poor characters if they are afeared they cannot digest another's influence and make it part of their own artistic flesh and blood. And worse still, if they imagine they haven't already got others' influences in every cell of their brains! In the pore of every ' I ' is ' We '.

A producer, taking this then as an axiom, would start to study what other artists in the past have done with, say, *Hamlet*. And that is where the difficulty starts. Where does one find the records of what others have done with *Hamlet* in the past? Alas, there are no such co-ordinated and readily accessible records! There are only scattered bits and pieces, some larger, some smaller. There is, of course, the Variorum Shakespeare (and I have come across theatre actors and producers who have never heard of it), but valuable as this edition is, it consists mainly of writings from what I call the ' literary school '. That is, those critics and historians who studied Shakespeare as a poet, as a writer, not as a playwright and a player and a producer. In this two-volume *Hamlet*, there are about 270 pages of literary and philosophical criticism of the text and action from the earliest extant (1710) to date of publication (in my volume 1905); only fifteen pages on actors' interpretations; two and a half pages on costumes; nothing on production or scene design.

This overweighting on the side of literary criticism and history is typical and it is time the balance was restored. Plays are written to be played, and Shakespeare's above all. After all, he didn't even bother to have them printed! And in this respect I welcome Dr. Richard Flatter's recent book *Shakespeare's Producing Hand* and Ronald Watkin's *On Producing Shakespeare* in which this aspect of *production on a stage* is highly stressed.

We have divided the play into the usual acts and scenes, as in the Variorum edition. But it is important to remember that the original division in the First Folio had no descriptions of the scene. The play began: "Actus primus, Scœna prima, Enter Barnardo and Francisco, two Centinels", and then the dialogue followed. The addition of a description of the scene did not appear until Nicholas Rowe's edition in 1709.

INTRODUCTION

But Shakespeare tells us all we want to know about the scene in his dialogue, and on the Elizabethan stage, with its flexibility, the play flowed like a modern cinema film without even a fade-out, except the natural fading of the day towards twilight. But, alas, we have no pictures of those productions, and can only conjecture on paper as to their visual aspect. The earliest prints of any Shakespeare play are those of the Nicholas Rowe edition of 1709.[1] The earliest picture approaching a *Hamlet* scene as staged is in that edition. So that in any case, the five acts division is the normal thing for productions since the Restoration. From all sources, it appears that William Poel's productions were the most accurate reconstructions of Elizabethan productions yet attempted, and we have included a photograph in the appropriate place. But, alas, there are only too few in existence!

Since setting out on this work, it has become more and more clear how criminally neglected is the recording and documentation of British theatrical life, and of its finest productions. It is interesting to note that the only documented and detailed attempt to preserve all aspects of a British production for posterity was made by an American—Rosamond Gilder—in her *Record of a Performance of John Gielgud's Hamlet* (Methuen, 1937), yet in this almost unique book the visual aspect is sadly neglected, the documentation is practically all in words, words, words! Instead of each scene being documented either by photograph or designer's sketch, there are only four scenes in the whole book, and they are printed haphazardly without any relation to sequence. The rest are just close-up portraits and a costume design.

Everyone knows the problems involved and the margin of error in attempting to reconstruct visual forms from verbal description. And for a producer or scene-designer in research on play production, this is the weakest side, the most neglected and worst documented.

The producer, therefore, searching for Shakespeare productions will have a very difficult task to get any bird's-eye view of what producers have done with his plays since Shakespeare's day. Furthermore, there is a great deal of writing and very little of illustration, and in this respect our own country, alas, is far worse off than Europe. The great blessing of private enterprise in the theatre since Good King Charles's Golden Days has succeeded admirably in concentrating attention on the purely ephemeral financial and ballyhoo aspects to the detriment of more permanent recording of its artistic aspects. The State and Municipal Theatres of Europe have, at least, kept some recording of their history, as theatre museums, archives, paintings, books or governmental decrees. We have had no such theatres, and those of a (hitherto) unofficial national status, such as the Old Vic, because of their poverty-stricken existence, particularly in their early years, were even worse off than some leading managements, who, at least, have photographs made for publicity purposes! Such photographs, however, suffer accordingly, and can often give a wrong impression of the actual production, because the photographer usually tries, at the management's request, to make a well-composed glamorized photograph and, consequently, rearranges the characters in a different stage position to that actually taken in the production.

[1] The only contemporary illustration of a Shakespeare play is the drawing by Henry Peachum of "*TITUS ANDRONICUS*" made in 1595.

Another factor is that the starring system, and particularly the influence of the cinema, has meant that the bulk of theatre photographs concentrate on the close-up and portraits of actors only, whereas to the theatre student, it is the long-shot of the whole scene in action which helps him to re-imagine the production when it is no longer on the stage.

The artist, too, recording theatrical history on paper or canvas, can equally falsify for the purpose of his art, and it is difficult to tell, quite often, from a painting or engraving, what the stage was like in its actual theatrical setting. Take the drawings of Irving's productions, for example (for some reason he would have no photographs taken even of himself in many of his famous parts), or Forbes Robertson's first *Hamlet*, it is impossible to tell from them which was backcloth, which wings, which props and which the artist's imagination![1]

The true solution would be for a set of photographs to be taken with a miniature camera and a high-powered lens *during* a performance, recording every episode and sequence throughout the play, contact prints to be made and kept purely for historical and research purposes, letting the publicity and art photographers continue their normal work. Thus on twenty or thirty feet of 35 mm. film, for a small cost, could be kept a full visual record in film-strip as near as possible to the ciné-camera.

But this, of course, is only one aspect: parallel with the static visual should be preserved the following: the producer's own working copy of the play, with any notes, ground-plans and drawings; the stage manager's recording on his prompt-copy of the moves and business; the electrician's lighting cue-sheet and notes of the lights and colours used; the musical score (if any) properly cued; the original designs of the artists and final ground-plans, or at least photographs of them; any written work done by the actors during rehearsals; any recordings on gramophone discs or tape recorders or television news-reel; any films whether news-reel or documentary; any sound-tracks (such as those made on 35 mm. film for Gielgud's *Macbeth*, noises-off and music); any articles or interviews with producer, designer and actors; and of course all the write-ups in the Press and publications.

If this sounds impossible, all I can say is that many European theatres have been doing most of this for years. The Moscow Art Theatre, for example, publishes *all* the archives of the theatre, including producers' notebooks, such as that of *Othello* (published by Bles, London, 1948) or *The Seagull* (published by Dobsons, London, 1952) with the text on one side and the drawings for *mise en scène* and ground-plans and notes on the other. Apart from this the Art Theatre publishes a Year Book with black-and-white and coloured stage designs, memoirs, historical facts, letters and articles by everyone participating in its work; and finally, it makes a series of sound-films recording the work of outstanding actors, with extracts from the various roles they have played, how they made-up, how they approached the role, etc. This is pioneer scientific work of unique interest and one that every theatre worker should envy and try to emulate, whatever his politics. We can, at least, look after the archives already existing. The pioneer work was done by the late Mrs. Enthoven at the

---

[1] We have since traced, in private hands, a prompt copy of Irving's 1874 production, which includes water colour drawings of wings and backcloths for five sets, by Cuthbert and Craven, from which it is possible to reconstruct the settings for this production.

INTRODUCTION

Victoria and Albert Museum, but the collections in private hands should eventually be housed in the National Theatre, when it has its own building.

This work is but a humble contribution towards preserving and collating for students and posterity the productions of one play only of our great Shakespeare. It is our hope, if this is a success, to continue with his other plays, and then to pass on to other classics. We hope other countries will do the same with their great plays.

Now, however, as to the present work, we have dared to entitle it *Hamlet Through the Ages*, but, alas, our first illustration is 1709, just over a hundred years later than its first performance! We have also tried to collate reproductions from all over the world, but this, too, had very serious drawbacks, firstly, the aftermath of war, and such a war, meant, in Eastern Europe particularly, a great loss of archives through deliberate cold-blooded destruction by the Nazis. In Poland, for example, all Polish books, manuscripts, museum collections were to be used as *fuel* only, according to orders of the German High Command. And great was the loss thereby. Then came the problem of communication in the artificially divided East and West Europe. There was one advantage, however, with the Eastern Republics that the Governments were concerned with their cultural heritage and treasures, and thus we received willing help, photographs and information, at no cost, whereas Western Europe, still depending mostly on private organizations and private charity, wanted fees for everything far beyond our sterling means, and so certain countries are perforce sparsely represented.

In working, we first located all the *Hamlet* illustrations we could find, and this involved a thorough search of all books on *Hamlet* and the theatre in whatever languages they could be obtained, and a search of all existing theatre and photographic collections. The final selection of pictures to be used had to be fitted into the limitation and pattern of the book.

Then copies had to be made and classified. This, at first, caused us to pause. If we had a good set of one production, showing all the various scene changes, should they be put together in one sequence? Or should all the photographs be classified into Act I, Scene 1, and so on? This latter was eventually decided upon, as giving the best opportunity to study the changing styles and, at the same time, often unchanging stage business in chronological order. My original title for this series was "Comparative Scene Design" and that is what it is, only by comparison can things be judged, however odious it may sometimes be! The Ghost scene in particular is well-represented and worthy of study. The different mad Ophelias, too, are internationally representative; but to start drawing lessons from their juxtaposition would be another book added to the vast Shakespeare library—we will simply let the pictures speak for themselves, giving only basic captions, stating (wherever possible) the country, the town, the theatre, the date, the character, the actor or actress, the producer, the scene and costume designer. Then in the text a minimum descriptive note to each photograph about the production and any special points of interest, particularly of an historical and factual nature. Finally, a synopsis of each scene which will enable the reader, almost at a glance, to realize the action that has to take place in the given setting.

Finally, I wish to pay tribute to that indefatigable theatre-loving pair,

Raymond Mander and Joe Mitchenson, without whose co-operation, patience and hard work this volume would never have been collected. The idea and conception were mine, but practically all the work was theirs. They are among those golden few who still labour for love, and who for the sake of their theatre collection have often forfeited financial gain, until it has grown and become one of the most valuable and comprehensive in private hands, and which they have willed to the nation—let this book be a tribute to such spirits all too rare in our commerce-ridden theatre.

HERBERT MARSHALL

THE TRAGEDY OF

HAMLET

Prince of Denmark

by
WILLIAM SHAKESPEARE

Dramatis Personae

CLAUDIUS, King of Denmark
HAMLET, Son to the late, and Nephew to the present King
FORTINBRAS, Prince of Norway
POLONIUS, Lord Chamberlain
HORATIO, Friend to Hamlet
LAERTES, Son to Polonius

VOLTIMAND ⎫
CORNELIUS ⎪
ROSENCRANTZ ⎬ Courtiers
GUILDENSTERN ⎪
OSRIC ⎪
A GENTLEMAN ⎭

A PRIEST

MARCELLUS ⎫ Officers
BERNARDO ⎭

FRANCISCO, A Soldier
REYNALDO, Servant to Polonius

PLAYERS ⎰ 1st Player: Player King
        ⎨ 2nd Player: Player Queen
        ⎪ 3rd Player: Lucianus
        ⎱ 4th Player: Prologue

TWO CLOWNS, Grave Diggers
A CAPTAIN
ENGLISH AMBASSADORS

GERTRUDE, Queen of Denmark and Mother to Hamlet
OPHELIA, Daughter to Polonius

Lords, Ladies, Officers, Soldiers, Messengers, and other Attendants

GHOST of Hamlet's Father

Act I Scene 1

ELSINORE. A PLATFORM BEFORE THE CASTLE

THE play begins at midnight on the ramparts of Kronborg Castle at Elsinore. Hamlet's friend, Horatio, has arranged to meet the two officers, Marcellus and Bernardo, in order to test the truth of their story of the Ghost's appearances, which he does not believe. As Bernardo is recounting the happenings of the previous night the Ghost again appears. Horatio, terror-struck by the sudden apparition, quickly masters himself and speaks to it. But the Ghost disappears. While Horatio is discussing the subject with his friends the Ghost returns, he addresses it once more, imploring it to speak, but the latter, though apparently about to do so, suddenly departs as the cock crows. The three men, trying to bar its way, lose their heads and strike at it with halberds, but the apparition, to mislead them, appears first in one place, then in another, and a moment later is gone. All three, overcome by the extraordinary occurrence, stay on, discussing tales concerning the strange power exercised over apparitions by cock-crow, until Horatio notices that dawn is near. They then break off with the suggestion that they should acquaint Prince Hamlet with what has taken place.

NOTES:

1 The Juvenile Drama Sheets consisting of backcloths and wings are almost certainly copied from a contemporary stage production. Many of the sheets of West are credited on them to a specific production. Unfortunately the *Hamlet* ones are not, but they can be taken as an adaptation for the toy stage of a live theatre production. The plates used for the illustrations are dated 1825 (see note, page 3).
    See also Nos. 11, 21, 167, 169, 196, 225 and 227.

2 The water-colour sketches by various scenic artists engaged on the Charles Kean revival at the Princess's are preserved in the Victoria and Albert Museum. They form a complete picture of the production as designed by Thomas Grieve. This was the first correct archaeological mounting, both in scenery and costumes (see Note No. 70). The play-bill of this production can be seen on the endpaper of this volume.
    See also Nos. 12, 22, 33, 36, 68, 105, 137, 151, 197, 226 and 228.

3 The five designs by William Telbin Snr. are preserved in the Victoria and Albert Museum. They are new settings for a revival in 1864 of Fechter's *Hamlet*, which he originally produced at the Princess's Theatre in 1861 (see No. 201). He was said to be the first actor to play the character in a fair wig (" a cross between golden and ginger "). He originally played the part clean-shaven, but in later revivals wore a small beard and moustache. In one of his many revivals he used the illusion known as ' Pepper's Ghost ' for the appearance and disappearance of the Ghost. Fechter was a Frenchman, and his broken English accent caused much comment in his day. He played the part in New York in 1870.
    Kate Terry was the Ophelia of the 1864 revival at the Lyceum. Nos. 3 and 35 may be alternative designs for the same set.
    See also Nos. 13, 35, 152 and 198.

4   Water-colour drawing of a full set showing backcloth and wings.

5   This is from a model of the set, showing actors as well as décor. Fuchs was the producer at the Künstler Theatre, Munich. He wrote a book, *The Revolution of the Theatre* (1909), which is well known on the Continent. It was written parallel to Craig's *Art of the Theatre*, reflecting a similar movement against naturalism, particularly in relation to the design of the stage and the setting. This, Fuchs the producer, carried out in association with the architect, Max Littman, and the designer, Fritz Erler, in the building and running of the Künstler Theatre, Munich. The settings were carried out by Adolf Linnebach.

6   A semi-permanent set with curtains and stylized arches used in various combinations. These settings were carried out by Adolf Linnebach.
    See also No. 234.

7   The first production of *Hamlet* in America was at Philadelphia in 1759 with Thomas Hallam, who also became the first New York Prince, on 26 November, 1761, at the New Theatre in Chappel Street. He had played the part in London " and was endured ! "

    The first American-born Hamlet was John Howard Payne, who played the part in 1809, when he was seventeen.

    New York saw the Hamlets of George Frederick Cooke (1810), Edmund Kean (1820), J. B. Booth (1821), Macready (1826), Charles Kean (1830) and Charles Kemble (1832). Mary Duff was the Ophelia to most of these and many other actors.

    The most famous American Hamlet of the nineteenth century was Edwin Booth, who first played the part in 1857, and took his farewell to New York in the same part, 4 April, 1891. He held the world record of 100 consecutive performances, 1864–5, until it was broken by Irving in London, 1874, with 200 performances, which remains to this day the longest run. The New York record was broken there by John Gielgud in 1936 (132 performances), equalled by Maurice Evans in 1945. The London runner-up for the title is Gielgud, 1934 (155 performances).

    Edwin Booth came to London and played Hamlet at the Princess's in 1880 (see page 94, also Note No. 176). Many foreign-language Hamlets visited New York, including Salvini and Rossi (in Italian), Daniel Bandmann and Ludwig Barney (in German).

    The Hamlet of George Jones, the self-styled " Count Johannes ", deserves mention. He first appeared in the part in 1836, and had a distinguished career as a leading man and in support of more famous actors. In his latter years he became increasingly eccentric, but continued to appear on the stage with disastrous results. When he played Hamlet at the Bowery Theatre, New York, in 1876, the theatre management, apprehensive of the reception he might meet, stretched a net across the stage, but not high enough to shield the " Count " from the vegetables aimed nightly from the gallery. A brisk trade in these missiles was done by the Bowery boys outside the theatre. The performance became a popular amusement, and was said to have attracted audiences away from Edwin Booth, who was reviving *Hamlet* at the same time.

    Another strange version of the play was acted in Pennsylvania (1855) as *The Grave Burst, or The Ghost's Piteous Tale of Horror*, with Laurence Barrett as the Prince, who also played many other parts in support of more famous Hamlets.

    For the twentieth-century Hamlets see : Walter Hampden (No. 7), John Barrymore (No. 17), Leslie Howard (Note No. 126), John Gielgud (No. 126), Maurice Evans (No. 133) and Raymond Massey (No. 62, 63 and 64).
    See also Nos. 95 and 158.

8   This was a clever production for a small stage and used a revolving unit (left), permanent rostrums and drop-cloths with curtains. Originally produced at the Arts Theatre, London, it was taken with a repertory on a Continental tour in 1945 (see No. 99), with Alec Clunes as Hamlet, Fay Compton as Gertrude and Jack Hawkins as Claudius.
    See also Nos. 20, 26, 99, 174 and 219.

9   This film, made by Cecil Hepworth for the Gaumont Company in 1913, had the same cast as the Drury Lane production for the farewell of Forbes Robertson earlier in the year. It was filmed at Walton-on-Thames during the summer. The castle for the Ghost scenes was built at Lulworth Cove, Dorset, at the, then, enormous cost of £400, and it took only two minutes screen time. The death of Ophelia was shot at Hurlingford-on-Thames, and

ACT I SCENE 1

the Graveyard scene at the Norman church in the grounds of Hartesbourne Manor, Hertfordshire (the home of Maxine Elliott, Forbes Robertson's sister-in-law). The cost of the film was £10,000, and it was " about a mile long ". It was shown at the New Gallery Kinema, Regent Street, on 22 September, 1913.

See also Nos. 48 and 49. For Forbes Robertson's stage productions see Note No. 107. There have been a number of other *Hamlet* films, among which may be noted :

(*a*) France, 1900. For the Paris Exposition of that year Marguerite Chan built one of the first sound cinemas (the Phono-cinema Theatre). For this Sarah Bernhardt made a film of the Duel scene with sound (the clash of swords) recorded on Edison cylinder records. It is believed other scenes were also included.

(*b*) France, 1907. Georges Méliès produced a film of the Ghost scene (an Italian version followed in 1908).

(*c*) France, 1910. The Lux Company produced a full-length version with Jacques Grétillat as Hamlet, directed by Henri Deffontaines (see No. 157).

(*d*) Denmark, 1911. Nordisk Films took the Royal Danish Theatre Company of Copenhagen to Kronberg Castle and filmed a version with Alwin Neuff as Hamlet and Emilie Sannon as Ophelia.

(*e*) England, 1910. Will Barker, a pioneer of British films, is claimed to have filmed the play in six hours with a fixed camera, before which sets, built one in front of the other, were moved away as the play proceeded, but we have not been able to substantiate this claim.

(*f*) U.S.A., 1914. The Vitagraph Company filmed *Hamlet* with James Young directing and playing the lead. Clara Kimble Young was the Ophelia. This is the only American version.

(*g*) Germany, 1920. Art Films presented a version of the Hamlet legend with Asta Nielsen, directed by Svend Gade (see No. 97).

10 The latest version of *Hamlet* made in England in 1948 was the first full-length sound version. It was made by Two Cities Films at Denham with Laurence Olivier as Hamlet. He also directed the film. The adaptation was made by Alan Dent and the music composed by William Walton.

See also Nos. 88, 142, 166, 191, 223 and 246.

Gramophone recordings of speeches from *Hamlet* cover all the soliloquies, among which should be noted : Forbes Robertson, Ben Greet, John Barrymore, Henry Ainley, Alexander Moissi, John Gielgud, Maurice Evans, Laurence Olivier. All these recordings except those of Ben Greet and Maurice Evans have been available in this country.

NOTE ON THE JUVENILE DRAMA SHEETS

The date 1825 on the scenery sheets of West has been found to be that of a reissue of the sheets. It was the habit of the publisher to put a new date on the old plates when reprinting. A scene dated 1815 has been brought to our notice by M. W. Stone, the authority on Juvenile Drama. He has also made the discovery of a sheet of Characters published by Jameson dated Nov. 13th (no year), and this has the names of the actors who played the parts printed on it. The costumes, etc., are identical with those on the West sheets of Characters, the earliest of which is dated 1819 (though this date is obviously a reissue date). The Cast is that of the revival of Hamlet at Drury Lane on 24 October, 1816, with Edmund Kean.

It is known that the Scenery was drawn by C. Tomkins and originally issued with small characters (though none of these appear to have survived), and if the 1815 date is correct, together they represented the first revival of *Hamlet* with Kean at Drury Lane on 12 March, 1814 (see Note No. 31). That the same set of Scenes was used in 1816 with large characters at the time of the second revival is now established. It is more than likely that the same scenery was also used at Drury Lane for each production; thus we now get a complete record of the settings for an 1815 production.

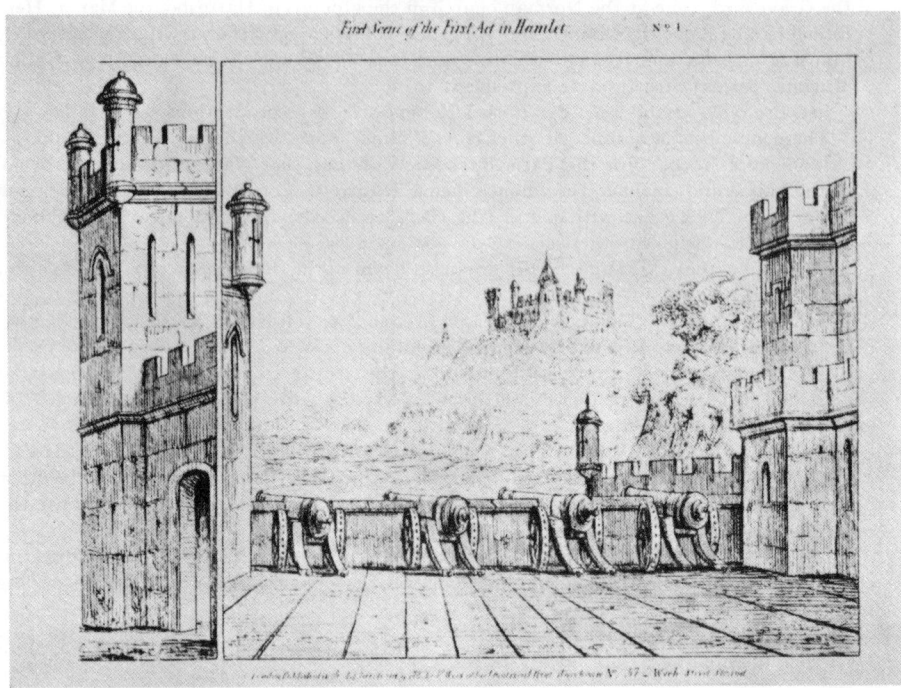

1 Juvenile Drama Scene, published by West, London, 1815. Backcloth and wing.

2 London, Princess's Theatre, 1850. Set drawing by H. Cuthbert from a design by Thomas Grieve for Charles Kean's production.

ACT I SCENE 1

3 London, Lyceum Theatre, 1864. (Hamlet : Charles Fechter.) Set design by William Telbin, Snr.

4 Russia, Petrograd, Imperial Alexandrevsky Theatre, 1891. Set design by Heltzer.

5 Germany, Munich, Künstler Theater, 1909. Model of set by Fritz Erler. Produced by George Fuchs.

6 Germany, Dresden, Court Theatre, 1909. Produced by Ernst Lewinger, settings by Fritz Schumacher.

ACT I SCENE 1

7 America, New York, Hampden's Theatre, 1925. (Hamlet: Walter Hampden.) Set design by Claude Bragdon.

8 London, Arts Theatre, 1945. (Hamlet: Alec Clunes.) Produced by Judith Furse, settings by Michael Warre.

9 England, Film, Hepworth Studios, Walton-on-Thames, 1913. (Hamlet: Forbes Robertson.) Horatio: S. A. Cookson. Marcellus: Robert Atkins. Bernardo: Richard Andean. Ghost: Percy Rhodes. Directed by Cecil Hepworth.

10 England, Two Cities Film for the J. Arthur Rank Organization, 1948. (Hamlet: Laurence Olivier.) Horatio: Norman Wooland. Bernardo: Esmond Knight. Marcellus: Anthony Quayle. Directed by Laurence Olivier, settings and costumes by Roger Furse.

Act I Scene 2

A ROOM OF STATE IN THE CASTLE

(Often played as a Council Chamber or in the Hall of the Castle)

IN deliberate and striking contrast to the midnight apparition of the Ghost on the battlements is the pompous Council scene at the Danish Court, which follows, where the King, amidst his splendidly attired courtiers, makes a speech on the tasks awaiting his Government. He reviews broadly, and apparently without embarrassment or reserve, what might appear to imply a certain ambiguity in his position; namely that, although still mourning the recent death of his brother, he has formed a marriage alliance with that brother's widow. He sends Cornelius and Voltimand as his ambassadors to Norway. Towards Laertes, the son of Polonius, he is friendly and benevolent. Laertes, who is young and high-spirited, has decided to return to Paris against the wishes of his father. But on this occasion Claudius does not show himself to be despotic. Family bonds are sacred to him, and this is a matter best left to a father's authority. After he has graciously dismissed Laertes, he turns with what seems to be a special warmth to Hamlet and dwells on what is now their double relationship. Hamlet responds with a sarcastic play on words, spoken aside. When the King expresses concern at his dejection, Hamlet rudely twists his words. The Queen, his mother, intervenes; and without noticing the double meaning of Hamlet's short and still sarcastic rejoinder ("Ay, madam, it is common") now directed against her, she presses him further. But Hamlet's irritability is now only too plain. As his exposition has been made not without asperity, the King thinks it time to put in a quiet word emphatically supporting his consort's wish. He has heard of Hamlet's wish to return to Wittenberg, but as he would miss his presence at Court he begs him to renounce the plan. The Queen adds her petition to the King's. Hamlet thereupon gives way, addressing, as though it were a matter of course, his mother, thus disregarding his uncle's appeal to him. The King, however, takes no notice of his discourtesy, and goes on to speak of Hamlet's resolve as praiseworthy, much as one would humour a child that thinks itself ill-used. He adds that the Prince's decision to stay shall be celebrated by the discharge of cannon during the banquet.

It is in a despairing mood that Hamlet meets his friends, and welcomes them warmly, especially Horatio. Clearly he has not seen him for some time, and had believed him to be still in Wittenberg; he therefore asks him in surprise what has brought him to Court. The modest Horatio laughingly ascribes his coming to indolence. But Hamlet repeats the question, this time with a sarcastic allusion to the drinking customs that await Horatio at Court, and when his friend replies that he came to attend the late King's funeral, a fresh access of bitterness is roused in Hamlet. Horatio understands his mood, discreetly acknowledging that he is justified. Hamlet responds by giving vent to all his pent-up indignation in an outburst of bitter mockery that betrays how deeply wounded he has been. His mind is filled with thoughts of his father whose form is so vividly conjured up by his imagination, that, staring into vacancy, he almost believes he sees him. At all events he speaks of him in such a way that Horatio thinks for a moment that what Hamlet sees is more than an imaginary picture. Horatio does not comment on his mistake, which, however, gives him the cue he needs. Horatio tells him of the Ghost's appearance. Hamlet is very deeply perturbed. He cross-examines Horatio persistently, even inquires what was the hue and expression of the King's face. But with his usual reserve and distrust of others, he at once imposes silence on Horatio. There is really no logical reason for so doing, but his ever-growing suspicion of foul play leaves him no other choice.

NOTES:

11 See Note No. 1.

12 See Note No. 2.

13 See Note No. 3.

14 A typical production in the Henry Irving tradition followed by Forbes Robertson, Martin Harvey and Frank Benson among others.
See also No. 23.

Dr. Carl Hagemann was the director of the Court Theatre. He wrote a book, *The Art of the Theatre* (1912), in which he gave his aims for an ' ideal stage ' free from superfluous details. His *Hamlet* was staged, according to a contemporary account : " In the interior scenes the backcloth was a Gobelins tapestry, and for the exterior scenes a curved horizon semi-encircled the stage, while in front of this scenery with artistically conventional lines was used for the near distance. For the wings he used two immense pillar-like towers on each side, placed one behind the other, which remained during the whole piece. Their powerful upward lines gave an impression of great height and dignity to the scene. These towers were movable and turned on their own axes, and on them were hung banners, torches, etc., according to the requirements of the scene."

Only the most necessary furniture was used on a ' neutral ' floor in these ' ideal ' interiors, while all the time the important points of space and depth, and placidity, were kept clearly before the audience. On this stage *Hamlet* was given, with a single interval after the third act, the result being a triumphant success.
See also Nos. 44, 154 and 204.

16 See Note No. 9.

17 This setting was designed for the New York production by Arthur Hopkins in 1922 with John Barrymore. The London version of 1925 was reproduced by John Barrymore with the same setting, consisting of a permanent curtained arch and stairs. Front curtains were only used to indicate changes of scene when absolutely necessary.
See also Nos. 93, 115 and 189.

18 This was John Gielgud's second Hamlet. He first played the part at the Old Vic in 1930 (transferred later to the Queen's Theatre). It was produced by Harcourt Williams. The New Theatre, 1934, was Gielgud's first production of this play. The settings were by Motley, and consisted of a central unit which could be revolved and, in conjunction with curtains and draperies, made a varied and colourful change of scene. Gielgud's later Hamlets are : New York, 1936 (see No. 126), Lyceum, London, 1938 (see Note No. 56), Haymarket, 1944 (see also Nos. 168 and 222).
See also Nos. 54, 125, 140, 187, 214 and 238.

ACT I SCENE 2

19 This was the second London modern dress production, the first being at the Kingsway Theatre in 1925 (see Note No. 113). It was produced in its entirety and the text was based on the Dover Wilson readings. (For Guinness' second Hamlet see No. 248.)
   See also Nos. 61, 81, 83, 85, 217, 218 and 244.
   The following is a list of Old Vic Hamlets, since the foundation of the Shakesperean Company. *Hamlet* has been played in its entirety during most of the seasons since 1917.

   1914, 1915, 1916 William Stack (also at Old Vic Stratford Season, see Note No. 128).
   1917 Terence O'Brien.
   1918 Russell Thorndike. (He also played Hamlet at the Lyceum theatre, 1926, with Fay Compton as Ophelia.)
   1919 Eric Ross—Ernest Milton—Russell Thorndike.
   1920 Charles Warburton—Russell Thorndike.
   1921 Ernest Milton—Rupert Harvey. (Milton played Hamlet on the visit of the Company to Brussels in June 1921.)
   1922 Russell Thorndike.
   1923 Ernest Milton.
   1924 Ion Swinley (he was the Hamlet of the Old Vic Season at the New Oxford in this year), and Ernest Milton.
   1925 Ernest Milton. (See page 18.)
   1927 Baliol Holloway. (Duncan Yarrow played for one performance.)
   1928 Ernest Milton.
   1929 John Laurie. (Also at Stratford, see Note No. 128. He played Claudius to the Hamlet of Esmé Percy at the Court Theatre, 1930. See also Note No. 183.)
   1930 John Gielgud. (See Note No. 18.)
   1932 Robert Speaight and Robert Harris. (See also Note No. 60.)
   1935 Maurice Evans. (Marius Goring played at the performances of the Short Version, see also No. 133.)
   1937 Laurence Olivier. (See No. 127; also at Elsinore, see No. 55.)
   1939 Alec Guinness. (See also No. 246.)
   1944 Robert Helpmann. (Old Vic Company at New Theatre, see No. 25; also at Stratford, see No. 136).
   1950 Michael Redgrave. (Old Vic Company at New Theatre, see No. 247; also at Elsinore, see No. 57.)
   1953 Richard Burton. (See page 153); also at Elsinore 1954. (See also page 153.)

20 See Note No. 8.

Edmund Kean as Hamlet, 1814. Act 1, Scene 5, "there is never a rogue in all Denmark but is an arrant knave".

11 Juvenile Drama Scene, published by West, London, 1815. Backcloth and wing.

12 London, Princess's Theatre, 1850. Set drawing by Jones from a design by Thomas Grieve for Charles Kean's production.

ACT I SCENE 2

13 London, Lyceum Theatre, 1864. (Hamlet: Charles Fechter.) Set design by William Telbin, Snr.

14 London, Adelphi Theatre, 1905. Hamlet: H. B. Irving. Claudius: Oscar Asche. Gertrude: Maud Milton. Produced by Oscar Asche, settings by Joseph Harker, costumes by Tom Heslewood.

15 Germany, Mannheim, Court Theatre, 1907. Set design by Dr. Carl Hagemann.

16 England, Film, Hepworth Studios, Walton-on-Thames, 1913. Hamlet: Forbes Robertson. Polonius: J. H. Barnes. Claudius: Walter Ringham. Gertrude: Adeline Bourne. Laertes: Alex Scott-Gatty. Directed by Cecil Hepworth.

ACT I SCENE 2

17 London, Haymarket Theatre, 1925. Hamlet: John Barrymore. Claudius: Malcolm Keen. Gertrude: Constance Collier. Polonius: Herbert Waring. Laertes: Ian Fleming. Produced by John Barrymore, settings by Robert Edmond Jones.

18 London, New Theatre, 1934. Hamlet: John Gielgud. Claudius: Frank Vosper. Gertrude: Laura Cowie. Laertes: Glen Byam Shaw. Polonius: George Howe. Produced by John Gielgud, settings and costumes by Motley.

19 London, The Old Vic, 1938. Hamlet: Alec Guinness. Claudius: Andrew Cruickshank. Gertrude: Veronica Turleigh. Polonius: O. B. Clarence. Laertes: Anthony Quayle. Produced by Tyrone Guthrie, settings and costumes by Roger Furse.

20 London, Arts Theatre, 1945. (Hamlet: Alec Clunes.) Produced by Judith Furse, settings by Michael Warre.

Act I Scene 3

A ROOM IN POLONIUS'S HOUSE

(This and Act II Scene 1 are combined in the usual acting versions)

THE next scene is concerned with the exposition of Hamlet's relations with Ophelia. It comes out through the warning given her by her brother, Laertes, in a farewell scene between them, that she has an admirer in the Prince. Laertes, who it seems has a sober and sceptical view of life, distrusts Hamlet's advances to his sister and tells her that her reputation may be only too easily endangered because the Prince, tied as he is by considerations of State, is not his own master in the question of marriage. She accepts his further warning submissively and with no sign that she is hurt.

The conversation between Ophelia and Laertes is interrupted by Polonius who, surprised to find that his son has not yet started on his journey, bids him make haste but all the same finds time to give him his farewell blessing in the form of a number of moral maxims. He takes his daughter Ophelia to task. It clearly costs him nothing to press his daughter to reveal the secrets of her heart; on the contrary he appears to take a certain satisfaction in so doing, picturing himself as a benevolent parent while in fact behaving as a petty and quarrelsome family tyrant. He contemptuously dismisses the idea that Hamlet's love can be genuine, and treats his daughter's answers as childish and futile. But when Ophelia emphasizes the fact that Hamlet has approached her in honourable fashion, most solemnly giving expression to his love, Polonius scornfully cuts her short with a further display of wordly wisdom. He even attempts to prejudice his daughter against the Prince by giving her to understand that she should not treat him with kindness, as he is simply taking advantage of his privileged position. This is a distortion of the truth, but a father's authority over his daughter is so absolute that Ophelia unquestioningly obeys his commands to sever all connection whatsoever with Hamlet.

NOTES:

21 See Note No. 1.
22 See Note No. 2.
23 See Note No. 14.
24 The Oxford University Dramatic Society (The O.U.D.S.), founded in 1885, gives productions of a very high standard. Many of the actors later become members of the profession. The Hamlet of this production, Peter Glenville, is now a successful actor and producer. The ladies of the cast are usually professional actresses. This play was again their choice for the 1952 Season.
    See also No. 80.
25 This was Tyrone Guthrie's second production of *Hamlet* for the Old Vic, the first being the modern dress production of 1938 (see Note No. 19). The setting was a large permanent

set used throughout with additions. It is interesting to compare the use of the same business in both modern and costume versions (see Nos. 85 and 86). Robert Helpmann is unique in having played the part in both the play and the ballet version of his own creation (see No. 248). He also played Hamlet at Stratford, 1948 (see No. 136).

See also Nos. 84, 86, 165 and 221.

26 See Note No. 8.

Ernest Milton as Hamlet. The Old Vic Company, London, 1925. (See Note No. 19.)

ACT I SCENE 3

21 Juvenile Drama Scene, published by West, London, 1815. Backcloth.

22 London, Princess's Theatre, 1850. Set drawing by H. Cuthbert from a design by Thomas Grieve for Charles Kean's production.

23 London, Adelphi Theatre, 1905. (Hamlet: H. B. Irving.) Ophelia: Lily Brayton. Polonius: Lyall Swete. Produced by Oscar Asche, settings by Joseph Harker, costumes by Tom Heslewood.

24 England, Oxford, New Theatre. (Oxford University Dramatic Society, 1935.) (Hamlet: Peter Glenville.) Polonius: Joseph Adamson. Produced by Nevill Coghill, settings and costumes by Richard Buckle.

ACT I SCENE 3

25 London, New Theatre (Old Vic Company), 1944. (Hamlet: Robert Helpmann.) Polonius: Lawrence Hanray. Laertes: Geoffrey Toone. Ophelia: Pamela Browne. Produced by Tyrone Guthrie and Michael Benthall, settings and costumes by Leslie Hurry.

26 London, Arts Theatre, 1945. (Hamlet: Alec Clunes.) Produced by Judith Furse, settings by Michael Warre.

Act I Scenes 4 and 5

THE PLATFORM, AND ANOTHER PART OF PLATFORM
(These scenes are played consecutively)

THIS scene is again the battlements. It is cold and near midnight, in the distance is a noise of revelry, heard from within the castle, together with the sound of trumpets and cannon. Outside, for those on guard, it seems all the more quiet, as with Hamlet now among them, they await the coming of the Ghost. Their conversation naturally turns to what is happening in the castle, and Hamlet tells them how the King is carousing, he couples his remarks about the damaging effects of this custom on the reputation of the Danes with the thought that a comparatively small fault may often rob a man of everything to which his great capacities entitle him.

Suddenly the Ghost appears, putting an end to their talk. Although expected, the apparition has a tremendous effect. Hamlet's reaction is violent; he cries out as if horror had stopped his heart from beating. But in Hamlet reason always retains a certain ascendancy and even at times of great spiritual stress he does not wholly lose his scepticism. In spite of his excitement he therefore attempts to give his words with which he next addresses the Ghost a certain objectivity. What is the meaning of this visitation? Yet his heart is not in these questionings, he feels drawn towards his father's spirit and turns to him with fervour. The Ghost must speak; nothing on earth is so important as that.

He is so carried away in spite of his urgent questions to his father, that his companions have twice to call his attention to the fact that the Ghost is beckoning him to follow. They warn him not to do so, but Hamlet does not hesitate. He pays no heed to the anxious warnings of Horatio, who fears for the Prince's reason if the Ghost should lead him to the edge of the cliff standing high above the seashore. Hamlet, however, has a presentiment that he is in the presence of his fate. And, when his companions, alarmed at the emotional stress under which he is labouring, make a well-meaning attempt to hold him back, he threatens them with violence, declaring with a levity born of horror, that he will make a ghost of him that 'lets' him.

Hamlet is now alone with the Ghost, who begins to speak to him. He can only hint at the suffering he has had to endure, but the little he says has an overwhelming effect on Hamlet. The Ghost then discloses the secret of the crime of which he has been the victim, and Hamlet, who has always been troubled by suspicions, is struck to the heart and filled with a burning passion for revenge. The details that the Ghost gives of his murder add fuel to the flames. It is true that in awakening all that is noble in his son's nature he gives no expression to his affection for him, his suffering is too great, but there is an underlying tenderness in the words with which he ends his sorrowful and fervent farewell, "Adieu, adieu! Hamlet, remember me."

Deeply moved Hamlet responds with a passionate cry. The Ghost has vanished. Conscious only of the desire to carry out his father's wishes he vows

ACT I SCENES 4 AND 5

in his ardour that nothing else shall have any meaning for him, nothing but this occupy his thoughts. He then turns to the question of his mother, and his step-father. For the former he has only a word or two of abhorrence; all his wrath is directed against the King.

The rest of the scene shows him still under the influence of his terrifying experience. His natural reserve prompts him to betray nothing of what he has learned, so that no one shall share the secret. In his friends' presence, therefore, he seems to make light of what has occurred, pretends things are not so ill with him and fools his companions by allowing the sentence, that seemed about to reveal the truth, to end in an empty jest. And when Horatio shows certain annoyance at this Hamlet readily agrees with him; not in order to give him any inkling of what has happened, but to take his leave with one of those superficial general observations that tell no one anything. In the 'cellarage' scene which follows, his conduct in forcing his friends to swear secrecy is therefore less surprising. But to this an unexpected and gruesome turn is given, for the Ghost suddenly takes part in the administration of the oaths, and, in a muffled voice from underground, admonishes those who are about to swear. Nevertheless, Hamlet does not give up the role he has assumed. Whilst nervous anxiety at what is heard, but not seen, drives him more than once from a place beneath which the Ghost is audible he jests before his friends with pretended gaiety at the strange listener, whose secret he refuses to betray.

NOTES:

27 This interior of the Theatre Royal, Orchard Street, Bath, shows an audience watching a production of the play. The setting consists of stock wings and a blackcloth and contemporary clothes. *c.* 1750.

28 Garrick first played Hamlet in 1742, and continued throughout his career to appear in contemporary clothes as was the custom. This print by McArdell from a painting by Benjamin Wilson was published in 1754.

29 This print, a magazine illustration of 1782, may be imaginary, but it shows the usual contemporary costume as used on the stage.

30 The outline drawings of Macready's production are from Sir George Scharf's *Scenic Recollections of the Covent Garden Theatre*, 1838–9. Macready first played in London in 1821.
See also Nos. 104 and 230. For other later Macready productions see Nos. 32 and 149.

31 Edmund Kean used a then fashionable "theatrical" Elizabethan costume, which followed the traditional contemporary dressing of the part. See also No. 66 and Note, page 3.

32 A later Macready production during his season at the Haymarket Theatre.
See also No. 149.

33 See Note No. 2.

34 The design is reproduced from a water-colour in the collection of Dr. Carl Niessen.

35 See Note No. 3.

36 In 1849 Charles Kean was appointed by Queen Victoria "Master of the Revels", and as such he was responsible for the annual dramatic performances in the Rubens Room at Windsor Castle. The scenery was a copy on a smaller scale of his London productions. His scenic designer was Thomas Grieve.
The original water-colour from which the title-page of "The Complete History of Theatrical Entertainments at the English Court", edited by J. K. Chapman, 1849, was engraved, is inserted in the copy of the book in the Royal Library at Windsor and is here reproduced for the first time by gracious permission of H.M. the Queen.
Kean first played Hamlet in London at Covent Garden in 1833, and the part continued in his repertoire throughout his career. After his official retirement from the Princess's Theatre in 1859, he continued to play Hamlet in London, the provinces, and during his

tour of Australia and America. He gave three farewell performances of the part at the Princess's in June 1866.

See also Note No. 2.

37 The *Hamlet* opera by Mercadanti to a libretto by Romani was produced at La Scala, Milan, in 1822. The placing of this scene in a crypt was followed in Leslie Howard's *Hamlet*, New York, 1936, which he also produced.

38 The *Hamlet* opera by Ambrose Thomas to a libretto by Barbier and Caré was first produced at the Paris Opera in 1868, and in London, at Covent Garden (in German) 1869, with Christine Neilson and Charles Santley. The drawing is from a contemporary magazine. There are also symphonic poems on *Hamlet* by Liszt, 1859, and Edward German, 1897. Tchaikovsky wrote a Fantasia Overture and incidental music for *Hamlet*, 1891. This Overture is used for the Helpmann Ballet (see Note No. 250). Ballet Music, Boris Blacher (see Note No. 250).

39 William Creswick managed the Surrey Theatre from 1849 to 1862 and established in South London a theatre similar to Sadler's Wells under Phelps. (They exchanged visits to each other's theatres on several occasions.) He played Hamlet a number of times during his seasons.

40 Alice Marriott first played Hamlet at the Marylebone Theatre in 1861. She commenced her management of Sadler's Wells in 1863, and again played the part the following year. She also made her debut in New York in the same character in 1869. The claim to be the first female Hamlet seems to belong to Mrs. Siddons (see Note No. 193), though only in the provinces from 1777. Her example was soon followed by her friend Mrs. Inchbald, who played the part at the Theatre Royal, York, on 8 April, 1780.

The first actress that played the part in London appears to be Jane Powell, at Drury Lane on 12 May, 1796, although no such contemporary claim was made. There have been many other female interpreters of the part, both in this country and abroad. Mrs. Bartley in New York (1819) is the first American woman Hamlet, others following thick and fast. The famous American " male " actress, Charlotte Cushman, played the part in 1851, and Eva Le Gallienne in 1937. When Julia Glover played the part at the Lyceum in 1821 for her Benefit, Edmund Kean, who had witnessed the performance, went behind after the first Act, and grasping Mrs. Glover by both hands, impulsively ejaculated : " Excellent ! Excellent ! " To which the quick-witted lady made reply, " Away, you flatterer ! You come in mockery, to scorn and scoff at our solemnity ! "

Julia Glover also played Falstaff, without, it is said unkindly, the need of padding.

Sarah Bernhardt played the part (see No. 73).

Late nineteenth-century Hamlets include Mrs. Bandmann-Palmer (over 1,000 performances of the character in the provinces from 1895) ; Clara Howard (Mrs. George Daventry) at the Imperial Theatre, 1899, and at the Pavilion, Mile End Road. This production was played as a melodrama with an almost continuous background of music. In recent years Esmé Beringer played the part at the Arts Theatre (1938).

Other unusual Hamlets include the so-called " Dog Hamlet " of the first half of the nineteenth century. These performances at the minor theatres, such as the Standard, Shoreditch, and the City of London, were often seen at Benefits. Tom Matthews the Clown and W. W. Lacy played this condensed canine version—which included a talented dog in its cast. This dog accompanied Hamlet during the course of the play and in the final scene the highly trained animal would be let loose at the guilty Claudius, almost pinning him to the earth while Hamlet killed him. It should be remembered that at this period a number of melodramas featuring dogs were being performed, so that a talented dog was not a rarity in a company.

Another strange performance is recorded on an old play-bill :

KILKENNY THEATRE ROYAL
By His Majesty's Company of Comedians.
(The last night, because the Company go to-morrow to Waterford).
On Saturday, May 14, 1793.
Will be performed, by command of several respectable people in this learned metropolis, for the benefit of Mr. Kearns,
THE TRAGEDY OF HAMLET.
Originally written and composed by the celebrated Dan. Hayes of Limerick, and inserted in Shakespeare's works.

ACT I SCENES 4 AND 5 25

Hamlet by Mr. Kearns, (being his first appearance in that character) who, between the acts, will perform several solos on the patent bagpipes, which play two tunes at the same time.

Ophelia by Mrs. Prior, who will introduce several favourite airs in character particularly " The Lass of Richmond Hill " and " We'll all be unhappy together," from the reverend Mr. Dibdin's Oddities.

41 Henry Irving first played Hamlet at the Lyceum Theatre in 1874, with Isabel Bateman as Ophelia. He later revived it to inaugurate his own management at this theatre in 1878, when Ellen Terry joined his company as Ophelia (see No. 177). He included the play in his repertoire on his first visit to America in 1884. His first appearance as Hamlet was at Manchester in 1864, at the age of twenty-six. He was always of the opinion that an actor should be young when he first played the part. It is recorded that on being told that a well-known American actor was thinking of playing Hamlet at the Lyceum, he sent for him and inquired his age. On being told he was fifty, Irving remarked : " Fifty ! Good God, my boy. Good God ! A man of your time of life to play Hamlet ! How do you know you won't do yourself a grievous physical injury ? No man can stand the strain of playing Hamlet, unless he began before the age of thirty-five ! " The ages of famous Hamlets would be a rewarding study.

See also No. 72, and footnote page xiv of Introduction.

42 Frank Benson played Hamlet with his own company from its commencement in 1883. His first London season was at the old Globe Theatre, in 1889, during which he played Hamlet. From 1886 he was responsible for the Festival productions at Stratford-upon-Avon (*Hamlet* was the Birthday play for his first season). The production there in 1899, in its entirety, was seen in London at the Lyceum Theatre in 1900. It is this production which is illustrated. He continued to play Hamlet during his farewell tours up to 1932. On the last tour in 1933 Ion Swinley took over the part.

43 The aim of the Ernest Carpenter season at the Lyceum Theatre was to present popular melodrama and classics for the people. Matheson Lang was his leading man throughout. In this scene snow fell on the Elsinore battlements. See also Nos. 170, 186 and 205.

44 See No. 15.

45 Oto Kawakami was the founder and leader of the new school of acting in Japan and with his wife, Sada Yacco, he produced Japanese versions of *Hamlet*, *Othello* and plays by Ibsen, among others. With his company he visited America and Europe, in 1900 and again in 1903, playing in London on both occasions. In the Japanese version of *Hamlet* the text was altered to conform with the native thought and speech. It is set in Japan. Hamlet is named Toshimaru and Ophelia, Orive. It was dressed in contemporary European clothes.

Hamlet was also produced in China during the Second World War.

See also Nos. 109 and 178.

46 and 47 Craig's work at the Moscow Art Theatre is sufficiently well documented to need little comment. It was in this production that Craig's favourite screens were tried out to the full, and their failure, in practice, to live up to Craig's theory is discussed fully in Stanislavsky's *My Life and Art*. The ground-plan was included in the Moscow Art Theatre's Year Book for 1946. Unfortunately, no illustration of the elevation is available. The nearest approximation to it is that of Act V as originally published in *Towards a New Theatre*. Thorough documentary archives of this production exist in the Moscow Art Theatre, including a stenographic report of the discussions between Gordon Craig and Stanislavsky. Gordon Craig played Hamlet for six performances in place of Nutcombe Gould, with Ben Greet's company at the Olympic Theatre in 1897. Irving lent him his costume and dagger to wear on this occasion. See also Notes Nos. 74 and 110.

48 and 49 See Note No. 9.

50 Max Reinhardt produced *Hamlet* in Germany several times during his career, the one with Alexander Moissi being the most famous. (Moissi played also in the modern dress version in Vienna, see Note No. 75.) The publication of Gordon Craig's *The Art of the Theatre* (1905) in Germany soon made its influence felt particularly in the work of Reinhardt, though it must be remembered that Adolf Appia's *Music and Stage Setting* was published in Munich in 1899. See also Nos. 111, 155, 206, 207 and 235.

51 Two sketches for a permanent archway with rostrums and settings.

See also No. 138.

52 This production was seen for four performances at the Edinburgh Festival, 1948 (when this photograph was taken). A new translation of the play was made by André Gide, with music by Arthur Honegger.

53 The first production of *Hamlet* in Czechoslovakia after the First World War was in 1926, when a new presentation by Bohmil Stepanek was used for the first time. It caused a great controversy, as it was a modernistic translation, and up till then the one and only canonical translation was that by J. V. Sladek. The part of Hamlet was played by the leading Czech actor, Eduard Kohout, who, for the first year, alternated roles with Zyomimir Togoz, a Slovene; and the interesting thing was that he himself spoke the lines of his own Slovene language (translated by Ivan Cankar), and the rest of the cast continued to play in Czech, but afterwards Togoz mastered the Czech language and became a leading actor of the Czech National Theatre. This production was by the chief producer of the Prague National Theatre, Hugo Hilar (synonym for Bakule). The modern designs were by Vlastial Hofman and expressed the whole treatment of the translation and the production.

See also Nos. 119, 139, 211 and 239.

The first performance of *Hamlet* in Prague (when it was still Bohemia) was in German in 1776 at the theatre V. Kotcich. The first Czech translation was performed in 1796 at the Hibernian Theatre, Prague.

54 See Note No. 18.

55 The Elsinore Festival was started in 1937 and since then companies from various countries have been invited to perform at Kronborg castle, the home of the real Hamlet. The performances take place on an improvized stage in the courtyard. The first company to be invited was from the Old Vic in 1937, when Laurence Olivier played Hamlet and Vivien Leigh Ophelia. This was the Tyrone Guthrie production seen at the Old Vic the same year (see No. 127), with changes of cast, the set being adapted to the conditions.

Other visitors have been:

Gustaf Gründgens	1938	(See No. 98.) German Company from Staatliches Theater, Berlin.
John Gielgud	1939	(See No. 56.)
	1940–5	No Festival.
Hans Jacob Nilsen	1946	Norwegian Company from National Theatre, Oslo.
Erik Lindström	1947	Finnish Company from Svenska Theatre, Helsingfors.
	1948	No Festival.
Robert Breen	1949	American Company. Production originally seen at the State Theatre of Virginia.
Michael Redgrave	1950	(See No. 57.)
Ingemar Pallin	1951	Swedish Company from the State Theatre, Norrköping-Linköping.
Michael Mac Liammóir	1952	Dublin Gate Theatre Company.

The Dublin Gate Company first presented *Hamlet* with Mac Liammóir as the Prince and Hilton Edwards as Producer in their 1931/2 Season, and it has been revived over seven times since and included in the repertoire of their foreign tours. They presented it in London at the Westminster Theatre in 1935.

There was no Festival in 1953. Richard Burton 1954 Old Vic Company.

This was a version of the production seen at the Old Vic in 1953 (with the same Company). See picture page 153.

56 This production, on a specially designed stage for the open air, was seen in London on the stage of the Lyceum Theatre for six performances in 1939 as a farewell to the theatre before it was closed. The Ophelia was Fay Compton. Both the Ghost and Claudius were played by Jack Hawkins (see Note No. 18).

57 This is a version of the production previously seen at the New Theatre (see No. 247), in a new setting. It was the second visit of an Old Vic company to Elsinore.

58 See Nos. 78, 141, 159 and 208.

59 The Marlowe Dramatic Society is the Cambridge equivalent of the Oxford University Dramatic Society, but they play with an anonymous cast. It was founded in 1910. Their production of *Hamlet* in Regency dress has been revived on several occasions. The company works with its own designers and until 1930 the casts were all male.

60 This production had two Hamlets; both Robert Harris and Robert Speaight played the part. See also No. 124 and Note No. 19.

ACT I SCENES 4 AND 5   27

61 See Note No. 19.
62, 63 and 64   This shows the model of the set, and the producer's plan for the movement worked
    out, for trial, on a cork model and the final effect with actors.   The heads in the foreground
    are of members of the audience, showing the intimacy of this production.

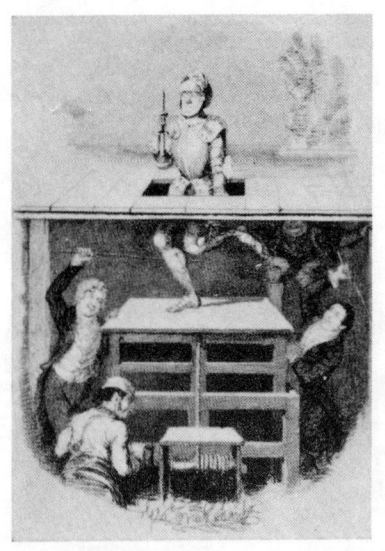

An etching by George Cruikshank illustrating an incident in *The Life and Enterprises of Robert Elliston* by George Raymond, London, 1844. It shows the use of the Trap for the Entrance of the Ghost in Act I, Scene 4.

London, Haymarket Theatre, 1807. Hamlet: Charles Young. See also No. 91.

London, Theatre Royal, Drury Lane, 1838. Hamlet: Charles Kean. (See Note No. 70 and page 104).

27 England, Bath, Theatre Royal, mid-eighteenth century. Interior showing Ghost scene with stock wings and backcloth.

28 London, Theatre Royal, Drury Lane. Hamlet: David Garrick.

29 An engraving by Walker after Mortimer, dated 1782. Probably based on the production at Drury Lane, 1780. Hamlet: John Bannister.

ACT I SCENES 4 AND 5

30 London, Covent Garden, 1838. Hamlet: William Charles Macready. Ghost: James Warde. Horatio: William Searle. Marcellus: Henry Howe. Produced by William Charles Macready.

31 London, Theatre Royal, Drury Lane, 1814. Hamlet: Edmund Kean.

32 London, Haymarket Theatre, 1849. Hamlet: William Charles Macready. Ghost: Mr. Stewart. Produced by William Charles Macready.

33 London, Princess's Theatre, 1850. Set drawing by Jones from a design by Thomas Grieve for Charles Kean's production.

34 Germany, Berlin, Court Theatre, 1873. Design by Lechner.

ACT I SCENES 4 AND 5

35 London, Lyceum Theatre, 1864. (Hamlet: Charles Fechter.) Set design by William Telbin, Snr.

36 England, Windsor Castle (Royal Command Performance), 1849. Hamlet: Charles Kean.
Special theatre and setting designed by Thomas Grieve.
From a water-colour in the Royal Collection at Windsor Castle, by gracious permission of H.M. the Queen.

37 Italy, Milan, La Scala, 1822. *Hamlet* opera by Mercadante. Set design by Alessandro Sanquirico.

38 France, Paris, Opera House, 1868. *Hamlet* opera by Ambroise Thomas. Settings by Rube and Chaperon. Hamlet: Faure. Ghost: David. Marcellus: Castlemary.

ACT I SCENES 4 AND 5

39 London, Surrey Theatre, 1849. Hamlet: William Creswick.

40 London, Sadler's Wells Theatre, 1864. Hamlet: Alice Marriott.

41 London, Lyceum Theatre, 1874. Hamlet: Henry Irving. Ghost: Tom Mead. Horatio: George Neville. Marcellus: Frank Clements. Produced by Henry Irving, settings by Hawes Craven.

42 London, Lyceum Theatre, 1900. Hamlet: Frank Benson. Horatio: Harcourt Williams. Ghost: Alfred Brydone. Produced by Frank Benson.

43 London, Lyceum Theatre, 1909. Hamlet: Matheson Lang. Ghost: Frederick Ross. Produced by Ernest Carpenter, settings by E. C. Nicholls.

ACT I SCENES 4 AND 5

44 Germany, Mannheim, Court Theatre, 1907. Set design by Dr. Carl Hagemann.

45 Japan, Tokio, 1891. (Hamlet: Ajiro Fujisawa.) Ghost: Oto Kawakami. Produced by Oto Kawakami.

46 Russia, Moscow, Art Theatre, 1911. Hamlet: Vassily Katchaloff. Produced by Stanislavsky, settings and costumes by E. Gordon Craig.

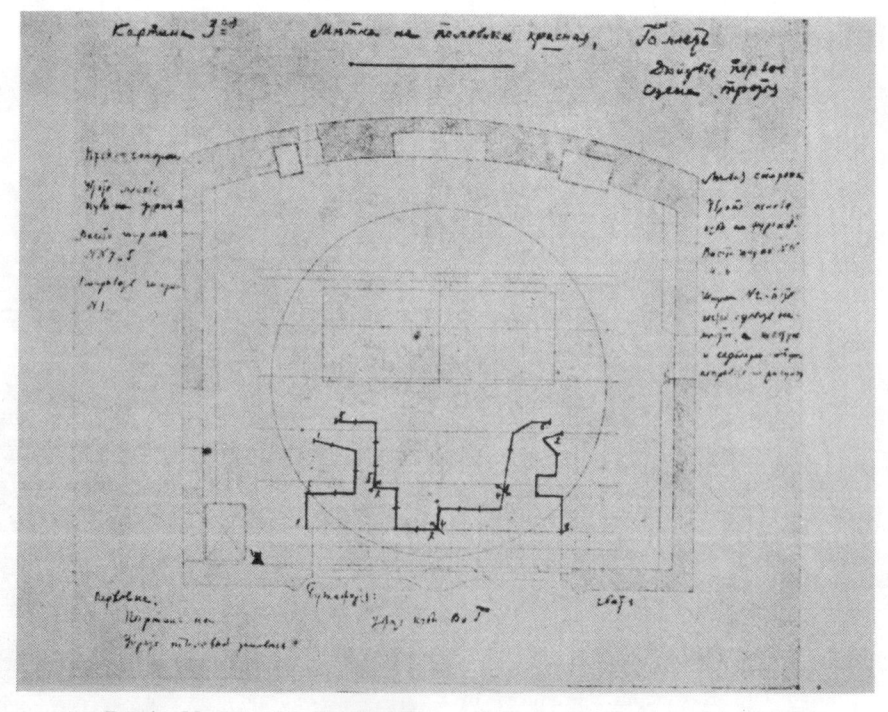

47 Russia, Moscow, Art Theatre, 1911. Ground plan by L. A. Sulerzhitsky.

ACT I SCENES 4 AND 5

48 England, Film, Hepworth Studios, Walton-on-Thames, 1913. Hamlet: Forbes Robertson. Horatio: S. A. Cookson. Marcellus: Robert Atkins. Ghost: Percy Rhodes. Directed by Cecil Hepworth.

49 England, Film, Hepworth Studios, Walton-on-Thames, 1913. Hamlet: Forbes Robertson. Directed by Cecil Hepworth.

50 Germany, Berlin, Deutsches Theater, 1909. Hamlet: Alexander Moissi. Horatio: Eduard von Winterstein. Ghost: Wilhelm Diegelmann. Produced by Max Reinhardt, settings by Ernst Stern.

51 Holland, Amsterdam, Municipal Theatre, 1918. Design by H. th. Wijdeveld.

ACT I SCENES 4 AND 5

52 France, Paris, Marigny Theatre, 1946. Hamlet: Jean-Louis Barrault. Horatio: Jean Desailly. Marcellus: Régis Outin. Produced by Jean-Louis Barrault, scenery and costumes by André Masson.

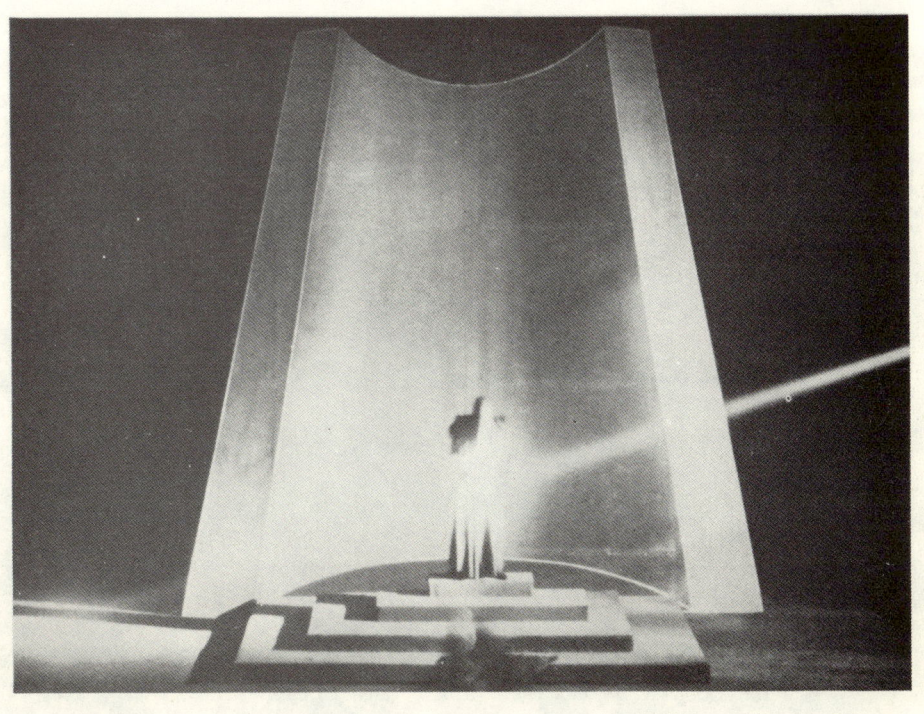

53 Czechoslovakia, Prague, National Theatre, 1926. Hamlet: Edward Kohout. Produced by Dr. K. H. H. Hilar, settings by Vlastial Hofman.

54 London, New Theatre, 1934. Hamlet: John Gielgud. Horatio: Jack Hawkins. Ghost: William Devlin. Produced by John Gielgud, settings and costumes by Motley.

55 Denmark, Elsinore, Kronborg Castle (Old Vic Company), 1937. Hamlet: Laurence Olivier. Horatio: Leo Genn. Bernardo: Owen Jones. Marcellus: Ernest Hare. Produced by Tyrone Guthrie, setting by Martin Battersby, costumes by Osborne Robinson.

ACT I SCENES 4 AND 5

56 Denmark, Elsinore, Kronborg Castle, 1939. Hamlet: John Gielgud. Ghost: Jack Hawkins. Marcellus: John Robinson. Horatio: Glen Byam Shaw. Produced by John Gielgud, setting and costumes by Motley.

57 Denmark, Elsinore, Kronborg Castle (Old Vic Company), 1950. Hamlet: Michael Redgrave. Horatio: Michael Aldridge. Marcellus: George Benson. Produced by Hugh Hunt, setting by Margaret Harris, costumes by Laurence Irving.

58 Poland, Warsaw, Polski Theatre, 1947. Hamlet: Marian Wrzykowski. Ghost: Wladyslaw Bracki. Produced by Arnold Szyffman, settings by Karol Frycz.

59 England, Cambridge, Marlowe Society (University Dramatic Society), 1936. Anonymous cast. Produced by George Rylands, settings by Geoffrey Wright.

ACT I SCENES 4 AND 5

60 London, Old Vic, 1932. Hamlet: Robert Harris. Ghost: Ralph Richardson. Produced by Harcourt Williams, settings and costumes by Owen P. Smyth.

61 London, Old Vic, 1938. Hamlet: Alec Guinness. Ghost: Malcolm Keen. Produced by Tyrone Guthrie, settings and costumes by Roger Furse.

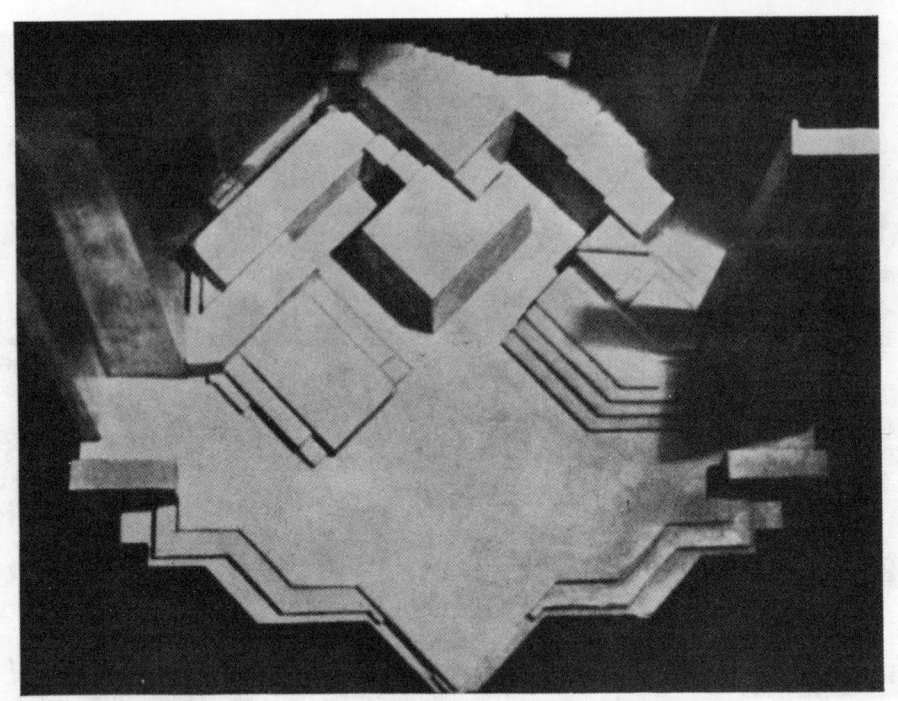

62 America, New York, Broadhurst Theatre, 1931. (Hamlet: Raymond Massey.) Production and setting by Norman Bel Geddes.

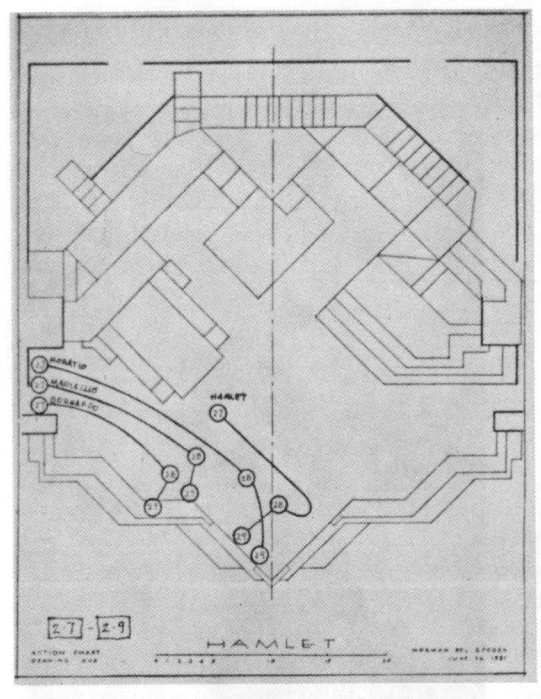

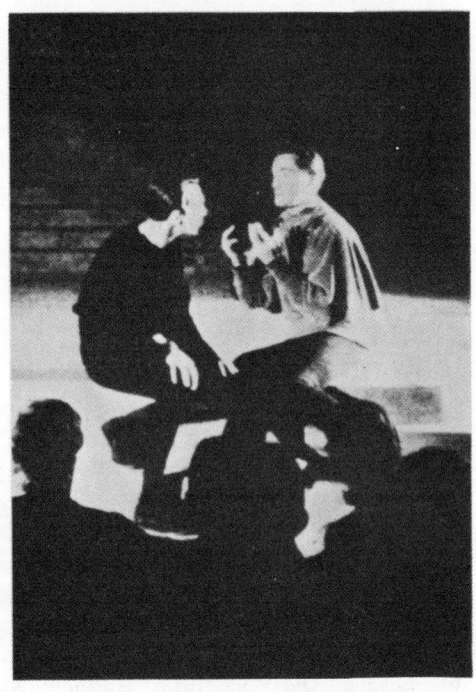

63 America, New York, Broadhurst Theatre, 1931. Production Chart.

64 America, New York, Broadhurst Theatre, 1931. Hamlet: Raymond Massey. Horatio: Léon Quartermaine.

Act II Scene 1

A ROOM IN POLONIUS'S HOUSE

(Usually combined with Act II Scene 2 in the acting versions)

POLONIUS is on the point of sending his son money and letters at the hands of an old and trusted retainer, and gives his instructions with long-winded complacency; but the argument, over-elaborated, proves too much for him and Reynaldo is forced to help him to pick up the thread.

This scene may be thought superfluous for the action but it probably has the object, apart from characterizing the Lord Chamberlain, of marking the passage of time. The sending of Reynaldo is intended to make it clear to the audience that some weeks have passed since the events previously witnessed. During the long interval Hamlet, who had sworn to the Ghost that he would revenge him straightway, has done nothing to carry out his vow.

At this point Ophelia, greatly upset, comes to tell her father that Hamlet has visited her in a state of apparent mental derangement. She describes how he had appeared before her. Polonius finds his daughter's tale in some ways not inopportune, for it gives him the key to a problem that has long caused much remark at the Court, to wit, the inexplicable distraction and lack of mental balance to be seen in the Prince. He is now convinced that an unhappy love affair has temporarily affected Hamlet's reason, and this belief is strengthened when Ophelia confirms his conjectures that the scene she has described had followed upon the breaking off of her relations with Hamlet, in compliance with her father's wishes. Polonius is not harsh by nature, and for a moment he shows himself honestly disturbed at not having believed in the sincerity of Hamlet's love and consequently at having wrought such havoc through the orders he has given his daughter. At the same time he sees at once that this will afford him a welcome opportunity of directing the King's attention towards himself.

Act II Scene 2

A ROOM IN THE CASTLE

(Usually played as a Council Chamber or in the Hall of the Castle)

MEANWHILE, as Hamlet appears to be mentally deranged, the King and Queen have summoned to Court two young nobles, friends of Hamlet, who bear the genuine Danish names of Rosencrantz and Guildenstern and to whom he was known to be much attached. The scene opens with their arrival. The King acquaints them, in his customary gracious manner, with the task he wishes them to undertake, begging them to try to distract the Prince, and, at the same time if possible, to find out what it is that so oppresses him. Neither of them can possibly guess that this apparent solicitude on the part of Hamlet's step-father, shared by the Queen, simply has the hidden object of discovering whether Hamlet knows anything of the King's guilt, and that they are both therefore merely tools in the hands of a criminal.

Hardly has their charge been given to them, than Polonius, bursting to make known his recent discovery to the King, announces the return of the ambassadors, Voltimand and Cornelius, from Norway, at the same time preparing him for what he has to tell him concerning Hamlet. This interests Claudius far more than any communications the ambassadors may have to make, and he asks to hear it at once, but Polonius delights to keep his questioner on tenterhooks by delaying a little longer what he has to say. This important State business of receiving the ambassadors must, he thinks, be transacted first; and then his news shall follow, like dessert at the end of a banquet; a remark in his usual bad taste. The King gives way, and the ambassadors thereupon make their report on the happy outcome of the conflict with Norway.

Polonius then has his say. His childish vanity and self-complacency prompt him to make as much as possible of this great opportunity of hearing himself address the royal pair. At last Polonius comes to the point and, to the great surprise of the Queen, produces a love letter addressed by Hamlet to Ophelia. The King is startled by this revelation. In order to judge its import he would like to know how far the love affair has gone. But Polonius takes up an attitude of exaggerated dignity, dwells on his own personal honesty, his devoted allegiance to the King and the authority he has over his daughter, proceeding to instruct his hearers, as one familiar with such things, about the various phases of the Prince's malady. Yet the cunning Claudius, in contrast to his rather foolish Queen, always easy to convince, will not accept the Lord Chamberlain's explanation so readily and demands further proofs. This naturally wounds the vanity of Polonius. But his eagerness in the King's interest is so great that he allows his view to be put to the proof in a way that does credit to his shrewdness; he will bring about, as if by chance, a meeting between the Prince and his daughter, at which he will play the eavesdropper with the King.

Before they can proceed with their design Hamlet comes in, reading a book. Polonius at once urges the others to leave him, and then turns officiously to the Prince in an attempt to test his mental state by bluntly asking if he recognizes him. Hamlet welcomes the chance to take advantage of his role of madman in order to give full rein to his dislike for the conceited and tedious old man. Polonius is completely deceived. What he hears only seems to support his diagnosis, he believes that there is no longer any doubt concerning Hamlet's mental condition. However, he would like to be doubly sure, and to gain time inquires what the Prince is reading. But Hamlet purposely misunderstands his questions and replies with a few paradoxical phrases and when at last he makes a pretence of giving him an answer to his question, it turns out to be no more than malicious invective directed to Polonius's senility. Yet his preconceived opinion as to Hamlet's madness remains unshaken. Polonius,

ACT II SCENE 2

seeing that he cannot prolong the conversation, and anxious to prepare for the meeting with Ophelia, takes leave most submissively of the Prince, though this politeness does not prevent Hamlet from again openly giving expression to his antipathy for the old man.

At this moment Rosencrantz and Guildenstern enter, taking Hamlet by surprise. Dropping his pretence of madness he greets his friends with a coarse quip such as may well pass amongst young men.

Rosencrantz, in an attempt to get to the bottom of Hamlet's melancholy, hints that he is suffering from unsatisfied ambition. The Prince, however, refutes this suggestion, in a characteristic self-explanatory passage. He then, however, breaks off quibbling by asking unexpectedly whether they will not accompany him to Court; and when he receives the polite reply that they will ' wait upon him ', that is accompany him, it pleases him to take this as though it means they will act as his servants. Only now, for the first time, does it occur to Hamlet to ask what has brought them to Court. The explanation that they give, that they have come solely on his account, meets with ironical thanks, and he continues to question them with great pertinacity, reading confession in their embarrassment. As they still withhold the truth from him, he reminds them with manifest warmth of their mutual love and friendship in days gone by, at the same time making it clear, in an aside, that he has lost all confidence in their loyalty. Rosencrantz and Guildenstern are taken by surprise, and seeing no help for it, confess. From this moment the bonds between them and Hamlet are broken. Although they are old friends, he makes no attempt to win them over to his side, the profound mistrust of mankind that has made him so secretive since the appearance of the Ghost—even towards his trusted friend Horatio—causes him at once to withdraw into his shell. He therefore gives them, instead of an explanation, a deliberately false account of himself. This exposition is cut short when he sees that it is greeted with smiles, to which his ready suspicion at once attaches a special significance. When he says that he has lost all delight in man (that is mankind) his friends appear to assume that he does not include women; but at once assure him that they were simply thinking of a troupe of players, of whose immediate arrival they have definite news.

Hamlet, who at the moment seems interested in anything but the task of revenge, receives the news with joy. He speculates on what may be expected of the actors and, with expert knowledge mixed with sarcasm, he passes in review the usual stock theatrical types of the time.

Polonius enters and Hamlet's mood promptly changes. He so dislikes the Lord Chamberlain that he cannot resist trying to make him look ridiculous, even though this involves playing the fool himself. Then the players themselves appear.

He is at once his old self again, greeting the players, whom he knows already, cordially and with no trace of condescension. He welcomes each one with friendly chaff and impatiently begs them to give some example of their powers at once in the form of a tragic speech. He then chooses a passage, about Hecuba, from an unsuccessful play which, as he modestly says, in both his opinion and that of those with expert knowledge, should not have failed. He remembers the speech so well that he can begin to declaim it. The First Player recites

E

it for him. He turns to Polonius to request that the players should be well lodged. Polonius's arrogant and self-righteous answer that they should be entertained according to their merits, he at once sharply rebukes. Only when he has done all he can for the comfort of these new guests does he take the First Player aside and arrange with him to insert a speech which he will compose himself of from twelve to sixteen lines into the text of a piece that they are to perform on the following day. He then dismisses them, giving a friendly warning not to mock Polonius; after which he takes leave of Rosencrantz and Guildenstern with formal politeness.

The second important soliloquy of the play (" O, what a rogue and peasant slave am I!") now follows. Hamlet's sigh of relief at being left alone is an indication of the repressed excitement aroused in him by the player's speech. It now breaks out. He realizes that he has unconsciously been false to his solemn oath to his father to concern himself with nothing but revenge, and has allowed his thoughts to wander from their allotted path. Now he is abruptly awakened from his dreaming by something directly connected with his father's murder, the player's emotion at the fate of Hecuba. He comes to a decision. Not indeed to compass his revenge, but at least to take an important preliminary step. And here a consideration enters for which the audience are not prepared: that the Ghost may have deceived him. In any case caution demands that this possibility be not overlooked. This is all the more necessary, because his examination of himself has not been without result. He knows that he is weak, even that he suffers from serious mental depression, and for those reasons is afraid that he may the more easily be made a victim of hellish arts. But he does not hesitate to trust his own faculties where the living are concerned. The effect of the play, with which on the morrow he intends to test the innocence of the King, should clear away any doubts concerning the truth of all that the Ghost has said, and the reliance he places on this pours oil on the troubled waters of his soul.

NOTES:

65 David Ross was a pupil of James Quinn and was engaged for Drury Lane by Garrick. For some time he managed the Edinburgh Theatre.

66 See Note No. 31.

67 Henry Erskine Johnston made his first London appearance as Hamlet in 1798 (see also No. 90). In Edinburgh he wore the traditional contemporary powdered wig, with a stage adaptation of Elizabethan clothes, as worn by Kemble, but in London he discarded the wig for his own hair.

68 See Note No. 2.

69 Barry Sullivan made his London debut as Hamlet at the Haymarket Theatre in 1852. He continued to play the part throughout his long career in the provinces until 1887.

70 Charles Kean first played Hamlet at Covent Garden in 1833 at the age of 22. When he made his great London success in the part at Drury Lane on 8 January 1838, he showed his taste for theatre costume reform, by discarding the usual stage Elizabethan breeches and substituting a tunic (see page 104). This costume soon became generally worn. With Kean's first full archaeological mounting of the play in 1850 the costume reached its ultimate form which remained the stock attire for Hamlet till the 1920's. This photograph was taken at the time of a revival at the Princess's Theatre in 1858.
    See Notes Nos. 2 and 148 and page 27.

ACT II SCENE 2

71 Mounet-Sully appeared in London with the Comédie Française when they gave a number of performances of *Hamlet* at Drury Lane Theatre in 1894. *Hamlet* was first produced in Paris at the Théâtre Français in 1769 in a version by Jean-Louis Dukis. The most recent Hamlet in Paris was Jean-Louis Barrault in a translation by André Gide. He was seen in this part at the Edinburgh Festival, 1948 (see No. 52). London has seen Hamlet in many foreign languages, among them Emil Devrient (in German), 1852; Salvini (in Italian), 1875; Rossi (in Italian), 1876; Bernhardt (in French), 1899 (see No. 73); Ruggero Ruggeri (in Italian), 1926; Moissi (in German), 1930; Minotis (in Greek), 1939 (the Gertrude was Katina Paxinou).

72 See Note No. 41.

73 Sarah Bernhardt first played Hamlet in Paris in 1899 in a new prose translation (she had played Ophelia during the early part of her career). She brought the production to London later the same year, and also gave performances at the Memorial Theatre, Stratford-upon-Avon. Monet-Sully is reported to have said of her performance, "Superb! A magnificent impersonation. It only lacks flybuttons."

An earlier French actress who played Hamlet was Madame Judith, 1867. There have also been women Hamlets in Germany and Italy.

74 This photograph is reproduced for the first time outside Russia.
See also Notes Nos. 46 and 110.

75 H. K. Ayliff, who produced the modern dress *Hamlet* at the Kingsway Theatre, 1925 (see No. 113), was invited to re-stage his production (in the German translation of Schlegel) in Vienna the following year with Alexander Moissi as Hamlet (see Note No. 50). The designs by Paul Shelving were the same as those used in London.
See also No. 203.

76 The influence of the London modern dress production of 1925 and its reproduction in Vienna, 1926, soon spread, and can be seen in the German production of the same year.

77 A new version of *Hamlet* in German was made and produced by Gerhart Hauptmann for Dresden 1927, but it did not supersede the Schlegel text which was and still is in general use.
See also Nos. 188 and 237.

78 See Note No. 58.

79 A highly original production in a mixture of modern and fantastic costume. Paul Bildt, the Polonius in this production, played the Ghost in the first revival of *Hamlet* in Germany after the Second World War (December, 1945), when it was produced by Gustav von Wangenheim at the Max Reinhardts Deutsches Theater, Berlin, with Horst Caspar as the Prince.
See also Nos. 117, 118 and 213.

80 See Note No. 24.

81 See Note No. 19. Andrew Cruickshank also played Claudius to the Hamlet of David Markham at the New Boltons Theatre in 1951.

82 This was the last *Hamlet* to be produced in the Soviet Union before the outbreak of war. It was revived in 1946.

83 See Note No. 19.

84 See Note No. 25.

85 See Note No. 19.

86 See Note No. 25.

87 There have been two translations of *Hamlet* and seven productions of the play at the Slovene National Theatre between 1899 and 1950.

88 See Note No. 10.

65 London, Covent Garden Theatre, 1757.
Hamlet: David Ross. From a painting by
John Zoffany in the Garrick Club.

66 London, Theatre Royal, Drury Lane, 1814.
Hamlet: Edmund Kean.

67 London, Covent Garden Theatre, 1798.
Hamlet: Henry Johnson.

ACT II SCENE 2

68 London, Princess's Theatre, 1850. Set drawing by Jones from a design by Thomas Grieve for Charles Kean's production.

69 London, Haymarket Theatre, 1852.
Hamlet: Barry Sullivan.

70 London, Princess's Theatre, 1858.
Hamlet: Charles Kean.

71 London, Theatre Royal, Drury Lane, 1893
Hamlet: Jean Mounet-Sully.

72 London, Lyceum Theatre, 1874. Hamlet: Henry Irving. Produced by Henry Irving, settings by Hawes Craven.

73 London, Adelphi Theatre, 1899. Hamlet: Sarah Bernhardt.

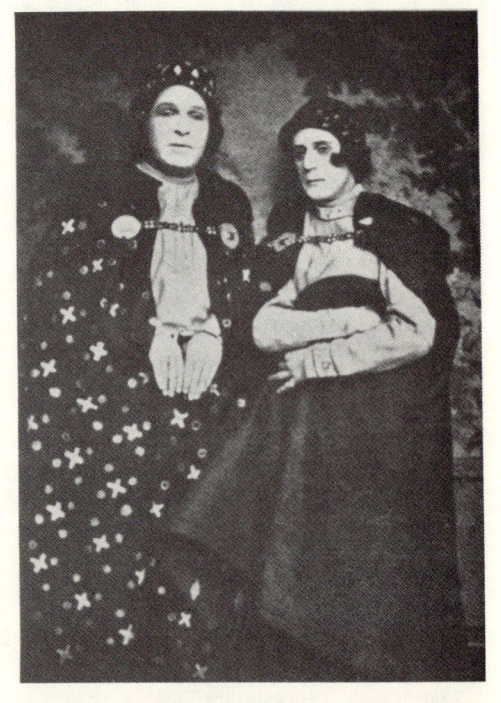

74 Russia, Moscow Art Theatre, 1911. (Hamlet: Vassily Katchaloff.) Rosencrantz: S. M. Komissarov. Guildenstern: V. I. Vasilyev. Produced by Stanislavsky, settings and costumes by E. Gordon Craig.

ACT II SCENE 2

75 Austria, Vienna, Deutsches Volkstheater, 1927. Hamlet: Alexander Moissi. Claudius: Franz Scharwenta. Gertrude: Freda Wagner. Polonius: Kurt Lessen. Produced by H. K. Ayliff, settings and costumes by Paul Shelving.

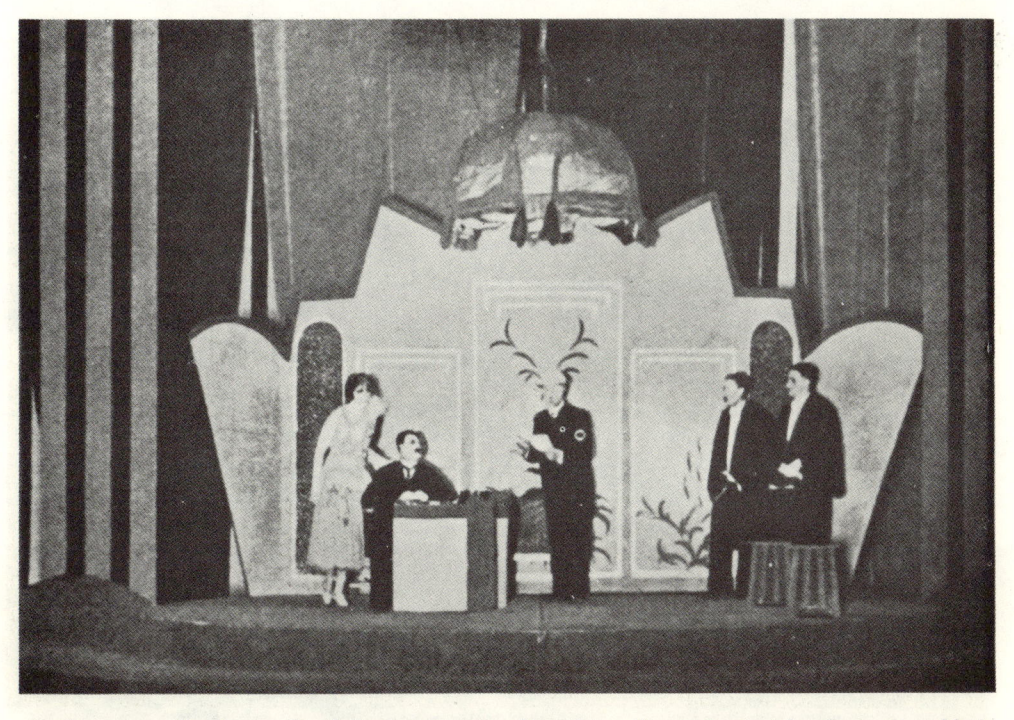

76 Germany, Hamburg, Thaliatheater, 1926. (Hamlet: Ernst Deutsch.) Gertrude: Maria Eis. Polonius: Lang. Claudius: Herbert Hübner. Cornelius: Lindt. Voltimand: Eggerth. Produced by Röbbeling.

77 Germany, Dresden State Theatre, 1927. Hamlet: Felix Steinböck. Polonius: Erich Ponto. Horatio: Paulsen. Rosencrantz: Klietch. Guildenstern: Nalsen. First Player: Decarli. Produced by Gerhart Hauptmann, settings by Adolf Mahnke.

78 Poland, Warsaw, Polski Theatre, 1947. Hamlet: Marian Wyrzykowski. Produced by Arnold Szyffman, settings by Karol Frycz.

ACT II SCENE 2

79 Germany, Berlin, State Theatre, 1927. (Hamlet: Fritz Kortner.) Claudius: Wäscher. Gertrude: Maria Koppenhöfer. Polonius: Paul Bildt. Ophelia: Blandine Ebinger. Rosencrantz: Weber. Guildenstern: Karma. Produced by Leopold Jessner, settings and costumes by Caspar Neher.

80 England, Oxford, New Theatre (Oxford University Dramatic Society), 1935. (Hamlet: Peter Glenville.) Gertrude: Isobel Scaife. Ophelia: Thea Holme. Claudius: John Wenzel. Rosencrantz: John Argles. Polonius: Joseph Adamson. Guildenstern: Richard Buckle. Produced by Nevill Coghill, settings and costumes by Richard Buckle.

81 London, Old Vic, 1938. (Hamlet: Alec Guiness.) Claudius: Andrew Cruickshank. Gertrude: Veronica Turleigh. Rosencrantz: Richard Wordsworth. Guildenstern: James Hoyle. Produced by Tyrone Guthrie, settings and costumes by Roger Furse.

82 U.S.S.R., Belorussia, Vitebsk, State Dramatic Theatre, 1946. (Hamlet: P. Molchanov.) Claudius: Zvezdochotov. Gertrude: Rodzyalovskaya. Produced by Valery Bebutov.

ACT II SCENE 2

83 London, Old Vic, 1938. Hamlet: Alec Guinness. Polonius: O. B. Clarence. First Player: Craighall Sherry. Player Queen: Freda Jackson. Produced by Tyrone Guthrie, settings and costumes by Roger Furse.

84 London, New Theatre (Old Vic Company), 1944. Hamlet: Robert Helpmann. First Player: Charles Deane. Produced by Tyrone Guthrie and Michael Benthall, settings and costumes by Leslie Hurry.

85 London, Old Vic, 1938, Hamlet: Alec Guinness. Produced by Tyrone Guthrie, settings and costumes by Roger Furse.

86 London, New Theatre (Old Vic Company), 1944. Hamlet: Robert Helpmann. Produced by Tyrone Guthrie and Michael Benthall, settings and costumes by Leslie Hurry.

ACT II SCENE 2

87 Yugoslavia, Ljubljana, National Theatre, 1948. Hamlet: Jan Slavro. Produced by Branko Gavelia, settings and costumes by V. Zedrinski.

88 England, Two Cities Film for the J. Arthur Rank Organization, 1948. Hamlet: Laurence Olivier. Polonius: Felix Aylmer. Directed by Laurence Olivier, settings and costumes by Roger Furse.

Act III Scene 1

A ROOM IN THE CASTLE
(Often played in the Hall of the Castle and run continuously into Scene 2)

Rosencrantz and Guildenstern present, to Claudius and Gertrude, a report on what they have so far accomplished. The King, whose shrewdness has, to a certain extent, penetrated Hamlet's disguise, cannot make much of what they tell him and he is therefore more ready to fall in with the plan that he and Polonius should conceal themselves and listen to a conversation between Hamlet and Ophelia. He, therefore, asks the Queen to leave them. She goes, and, after addressing some friendly words to Ophelia which hint that a happy end to all their differences may be brought about by her marriage with the Prince, Polonius proceeds to lay his trap for Hamlet. Ophelia is shown her place, instructed in her part, and given a prayer-book. She agrees to everything with her customary acquiescence, whilst Polonius—possibly on account of the part played in the venture by the prayer-book—saves his face with a few unctuous words of disapproval at such a parade of piety. The sleeping conscience of the King stirs unexpectedly, and for the first time, in an aside, he gives expression to a sense of guilt that has not hitherto been perceptible—the reason for this passage being, no doubt, that of removing any uncertainty that the audience may have felt after Hamlet's recently expressed scepticism as to the genuineness of the Ghost.

Hamlet now enters communing with himself, and weighing, one against the other, the relative values of life and death ("To be, or not to be").

The soliloquy comes to an end as Hamlet perceives Ophelia, apparently absorbed in her prayer-book; he greets her good-humouredly in momentary forgetfulness of his supposed madness. Ophelia seizes the opportunity of begging him to take back the presents he has previously given her, which now, owing to his change of attitude, have lost all value for her. But Hamlet pleads that he knows nothing of any presents. He has put Ophelia out of his mind and has abandoned himself to his melancholy and pessimism, which have turned him into an argumentative moralizer, hostile to women. He addresses her as though she were a stranger to him with half-rhetorical questions requiring no reply, and warns the astonished girl in characteristically didactic fashion that she should cling to her virtue, endangered (it seems to him) by her beauty, at a time when, as he knows from his own recent experience, corruption is rife. At all events his pessimism does not allow him to believe in women who are beautiful and at the same time virtuous: a distrust of female virtue which he has already shown in his words to Polonius concerning Ophelia. But the momentary impulse to revile himself gives way to a misanthropic reflection on the worthlessness of mankind, which in turn leads him to the conclusion that life should be denied; hence his advice to Ophelia to go into a nunnery.

The eavesdroppers now leave their hiding-place. They have no compunction at her grief or at the way in which they have used her as their tool. The

ACT III SCENE 1

King, who is no fool, has already drawn his own conclusions from what he has heard and has rejected Polonius's explanation. He has made up his mind : the Prince is dangerous. The situation can only be dealt with by some resolute course of action, such as sending him to England. But the obstinate Polonius counters this with a final proposal; that of persuading Hamlet's mother, after the play, to perform a similar part to that just undertaken by Ophelia, and to sound her son. The King agrees to this plan.

NOTES:

89 Stephen Kemble was the brother of John Philip Kemble, Charles Kemble and Mrs. Siddons. He managed Scottish theatres, including Edinburgh 1788, Aberdeen 1795, as well as making London appearances. He is usually remembered as the actor who could play Falstaff without padding. The caricature shows the traditional ' modern dress ', a black velvet Court dress with Orders of the Garter and Elephant and one ungartered stocking as worn by Garrick 1742, John Henderson 1777, and by all other actors until the reforms of John Philip Kemble in 1783 (see Note No. 148).

90 Henry Erskine Johnston, 'The Scottish Roscius', first appeared as Hamlet in Edinburgh in 1795 before he came to London to make his first appearance there in the same character. (The print illustrated is dated 1795.) He also played the part in New York, 1837 (see also No. 67).

91 Charles Mayne Young, an actor of the Kemble school, made his first London appearance as Hamlet in 1807 and took his farewell at Covent Garden, in the same character, in 1832 (Macready playing the Ghost) (see also page 27).
    This painting was titled as of Young and Mrs. Glover, and has often been reproduced as such until recent research has found that the original entry in the Museum Catalogue made in the 1860's was an error. It depicts Mrs. Glover's daughter Phillis Glover, who first played Ophelia to Young's Hamlet at Covent Garden in 1826. She last appeared with him in the part the following year. Clint most likely painted the picture at this time, though it was not exhibited at the Royal Academy until 1831 (the year in which Miss Glover died).

92 It is interesting to note that E. W. Godwin, the architect and designer who was responsible for the archaeology of this production, was the father of Gordon Craig and the grandfather of Edward Carrick. He used the beginning of the eleventh century, the period of the original story, for his inspiration, although Wilson Barrett dressed the character in the costume of a sixteenth-century German student from Wittenberg following the Talma tradition (see Note No. 148).

93 See Note No. 17.   94 A simple curtain setting with rostrums and screens.   95 See Note No. 7.

96 This production was planned, but we can find no record of its having taken place. The square columns, which were movable from the rostrums at the base, were used in various combinations.

97 This film was directed by Svend Gade, who was responsible for the designs of the Berlin *Hamlet* of 1910 (see No. 171). It was based not on Shakespeare's play, but on the old Danish legend of Princess Hamlet, who for reasons of state had to masquerade as a man. There is a romantic interest between the Princess and Horatio. Asta Nielsen, a Danish actress, made films both in her own country and Germany (see Note No. 9).

98 This *Hamlet*, produced in and for Nazi Germany, tried to express the back-to-the-primitive " alt deutsch " style in its costumes and settings and the iron will-to-power of the " master race " in its treatment of the character of Hamlet. Gustaf Gründgens and his company were invited to the Edinburgh Festival (1949) and gave performances of *Faust*. He played Hamlet at Elsinore in 1938 (see Note No. 55).

99 See Note 8.

100 This production by the Bristol Old Vic Company, 1948, was seen later in the same year at St. James's Theatre, London, with some changes of cast. William Devlin at the St. James's played Claudius and the Ghost.
    See also No. 135.

89 Hamlet: Stephen Kemble. A caricature by Robert Dighton, 1794.

90 Edinburgh, Theatre Royal, 1795. Hamlet: Henry Johnson.

91 London, Covent Garden Theatre, 1826. Hamlet: Charles Young. Ophelia: Phillis Glover. From a painting by George Clint in the Victoria and Albert Museum.

92 London, Princess's Theatre, 1884. Hamlet: Wilson Barrett. Ophelia: Mary Eastlake. Produced by Wilson Barrett, settings by Walter Hann. The archaeology of the play by E. W. Godwin.

ACT III SCENE 1

93 London, Haymarket Theatre, 1925. Hamlet: John Barrymore. Produced by John Barrymore, settings by Robert Edmond Jones

94 Hungary, Budapest, National Theatre, 1935. Model of setting by M. Varga.

95 America, New York, Hampden's Theatre, 1925. (Hamlet: Walter Hampden.) Set design by Claude Bragdon.

96 Austria, Vienna, Burgtheater, 1922. Set design by Oskar Strnad.

ACT III SCENE 1

97 Germany, Film, 1920. Hamlet: Asta Nielsen. Directed by Svend Gade.

98 Germany, Berlin, State Theatre, 1935. Hamlet: Gustaf Gründgens.

99 London, Arts Theatre Production. (Continental tour), 1945. Hamlet: Alec Clunes. Ophelia: Valerie Hanson. Produced by Judith Furse. Settings by Michael Warre. Costumes by Maisie Meiklejohn.

100 England, Bristol, Theatre Royal (Old Vic Company), 1948. Hamlet: Robert Eddison. Ophelia: Jane Wenham. Claudius: Alexander Gauge. Polonius: Paul Rogers. Produced by Hugh Hunt, settings and costumes by Alan Barlow.

Act III Scene 2

A HALL IN THE CASTLE

(This scene in the usual acting versions is run continuously on from the previous scene)

THE next scene shows Hamlet, once more in a normal mood, with the players, whom he instructs in their art. What is of chief importance to him is the presentation of passion, and he counsels them to handle this with restraint, recommending naturalness, objectivity and sincerity of feeling; which all accord with the drama's classic aim of being the mirror of reality. They are, however, warned against playing to the gallery, and against that exaggeration only pleasing to the ' unskilful ', and he finds words of biting criticism for gagging by the comedians.

When the players have listened to the advice offered them, they go out, and Hamlet calls Horatio, whom he has kept informed of all that has happened since the appearance of the Ghost, so that he can now help him to observe the King during the performance of the play.

The guests now arrive to witness the play, headed by the King who enters with a courteous word for Hamlet. But Hamlet will not respond to his friendly advances and repulses him with a bitter jest. A ribald witticism serves to snub Polonius after which Hamlet concerns himself entirely with Ophelia, behaving to her with that extraordinary lack of restraint in which, under his cloak of madness, he allows himself to indulge.

The merriment that Hamlet displays in his running commentary on the play is unbalanced and rancorous, while the fun he makes of the players with whom in reality he is so friendly, is simply in accordance with the part he is playing.

The performance begins with a dumb show intended to indicate the chief points of the action of the play that is to follow.

Hamlet's nervous anxiety can brook no delay. He has not concealed his impatience before the performance started, and is now anxious to assure himself of its effect on his mother; but the ingenuous Queen has not noticed the similarities, and answers the shrewd questions with which he hopes to trip her up with complete unconcern. The King, however, is disturbed and asks Hamlet—too late—to tell him more about the action. According to usual practice the title at least should have been announced at the beginning of the performance. This has not been done—apparently on purpose—for it is only now made public, immediately before the unmasking of the King. The scarcely concealed contempt with which he relates the story can hardly leave the King any longer in doubt, while the words and gestures employed by the player-murderer a moment later, must bring him to certainty. He has been discovered! With derisive triumph Hamlet at once repeats what he has already said: why should the King be disturbed? This is merely the history of the Duke Gonzago. But the King does not hear him; he is so upset that the Queen becomes alarmed

ACT III SCENE 2

and the Lord Chamberlain at once commands the performance to be broken off. The play is over; the company quickly disperses and only Hamlet, almost beside himself with excitement, remains with Horatio.

His earlier feelings of self-abasement and depression suddenly give place to the wildest exuberance. In his exultation he is impelled to give an outlet to his feelings by singing and leaping about, and calls for music to celebrate his success. When Rosencrantz and Guildenstern re-enter, he is so little able to control himself that he jeers patronizingly at the illness of the King, until Guildenstern, growing irritated, begs him not to behave in such a manner; to which Hamlet replies with bland politeness. Guildenstern appears hurt at this obvious attempt to fool him and threatens to withdraw. But a moment later when Rosencrantz delivers his message, containing a reproof from his mother, his mood changes again. At the thought of her his whole soul is filled with bitter contempt. Rosencrantz realizes that the Prince's secret is still undiscovered, and that his own task is not at an end.

Polonius now arrives on the scene, thereby only increasing Hamlet's irritation. Despite his excitement, he cannot deny himself the pleasure of making Polonius look foolish, and so leads him on into ludicrously servile agreements with him, on the subject of the various shapes he sees in the clouds. But on this occasion the comic interlude between the two is short, for Hamlet finds any company at the moment burdensome, and wishes to go to the Queen.

And so his will to act, though stronger than it has ever been since the appearance of the Ghost, is once again deflected. His triumph in unmasking the King has led to no practical decision. The mountain has laboured and brought forth a mouse. His principal task is forgotten.

NOTES:

101 This engraving is an illustration from a magazine *The Universal Museum*, 1730, and may be certainly taken to represent a stage presentation of the period, most probably with Robert Wilkes at Drury Lane.

101A John Henderson made his debut at Bath in 1772 as Hamlet. He later played the part during his first London season, at the Haymarket Theatre in 1777. He first played the part with Wilson as Polonius at Covent Garden Theatre in 1779.

102 *Hamlet* was first produced with any success in the German language by Friedrich Schröder in 1776 at Hamburg (there was a performance earlier in Vienna which completely failed). It had been acted in Hamburg as early as 1625 (in English) by a company of English players (see Note No. 183). The Döbbelin company in Berlin was one of the best of the few companies performing in Germany at this time. Its director, Karl Döbbelin, and his daughter played the Ghost and Ophelia. Johann Brockmann, who played Hamlet, had created the part in the original Hamburg production of 1776.
  See also No. 146.

103 The characters from the Juvenile Theatre version of the play by Hodgson were made as solo figures and the great moments of the play as tableaux. The solo figures being made to cut out, their background was partially imaginary and incidental. The figures were moved on slides and the tableaux used as drops. They are founded, without doubt, on a contemporary stage production.
  See also No. 229.

104 See Note No. 30.   105 See Note No. 2.

106 Beerbohm Tree first played Hamlet at the Haymarket Theatre in 1892. He revived it annually during his festivals at His Majesty's Theatre from 1905 to 1910. He also took

it in his repertoire on his visit to Berlin in 1907. In 1905 he played it without scenery (in a black curtain setting) when critics said his performance was seen at its best.

107 When Forbes Robertson played Hamlet at the Lyceum in 1897 he was lent most of his scenery by Henry Irving, who had his own production in store. The drawings by Hawes Craven (Nos. 153 and 185) are from the souvenir of the 1897 production. Forbes Robertson toured this production and revived it in London at the Lyric Theatre in 1902 (see No. 182). The photographs Nos. 107, 231 and 232 were taken at Drury Lane in 1913 on the occasion of Forbes Robertson's farewell season. (This was the production that was filmed, see Note No. 9.) He also took his company to Berlin (1898) and New York (1904), and played Hamlet.

108 Martin Harvey first played Hamlet in London at the Lyric Theatre in 1905. He revived it at His Majesty's Theatre in 1916, and at Covent Garden in 1919.
See also Nos. 112, 184, 209 and 233.

109 See Note No. 45.

110 See Note No. 46. This photograph is reproduced for the first time outside Russia.

111 See Note No. 50.

112 Martin Harvey was an artist of considerable talent and had absorbed the ideas of the more advanced of contemporary stage designers and producers. The revivals of *Hamlet* in 1916 and 1919 were wholly designed by him, on the methods of Reinhardt.

113 and 114 The production in Birmingham by Sir Barry Jackson's Repertory Company in 1925 was brought to the Kingsway Theatre the same year. (See Nos. 161, 210 and 236.) See also Note No. 75 for the production in Vienna.
Another modern dress production was staged by Herbert Prentice for the Repertory Company in 1935 with Stephen Murray as Hamlet.

115 See Note No. 17.

116 A reflection of the symbolistic conception of Craig set in an abstract Middle Ages, pompous and over-Gothic, half grey, half black; the whole treated as a gigantic mousetrap in the Castle.

117 and 118 See Note No. 79.

119 See Note No. 53.

120 The Georgian State Theatre was modelled on the lines of the Imperial Theatres of Petrograd and Moscow; since the Revolution this theatre has progressed and gained a world-wide reputation.

121 and 122 The year after the controversial production at the National Theatre, the Prague Municipal Theatre, known as the Vinohradsky Divadlo, presented *Hamlet* in a more conventional production, using an adaptation of the old translation by Sladek together with a much later translation by J. J. Kolař. The Sladek was a more classical and literary one, and not so suitable for playing as Kolař's, who was himself an actor. The next production of *Hamlet* in the Municipal Theatre was in 1941 under the Nazi occupation. Hamlet was played by Milos Nedbal, and there was a new translation by Erik Saudek. The producer was Bohus Stejskal and the settings were by Frantisek Troster. It is interesting that, owing to the heavy censorship, any possible allusions against State authorities were struck out. The theatre deliberately hid the fact that the translation was by Saudek, as he was a Jew, or the production would have instantly been forbidden. In order for him to receive his royalties it was announced as being by a ' pure ' Czech, Scoumel, who was embarrassed by the congratulations poured in on him for his brilliant translation. He had to learn the translation in both languages by heart, in order to be able to deal with any questions. One critic did dispute his authorship in the Press and claimed that it was Saudek. Fortunately, the Nazis never learned the truth.
See also Nos. 164, 173, 212 and 240.

123 This production was staged in aid of King George's Pension Fund for Actors for two special matinées at the Haymarket Theatre in 1930, with Henry Ainley as Hamlet. The same production was restaged, by Charles La Trobe for a run at the same theatre the following

ACT III SCENE 2

year with Godfrey Tearle as Hamlet and Fay Compton as Ophelia. Godfrey Tearle also played Hamlet for the Fellowship of Players in 1925.

124 See Note No. 60.

125 See Note No. 18.

126 New York had two Hamlets in 1936, as both John Gielgud and Leslie Howard played the part in different productions (Howard was his own producer). Gielgud played in New York for 132 performances, the longest run of the play on record in the States. (For other record runs see Note No. 7.) For John Gielgud's London Hamlets see Note No. 18.

127 This production of the Old Vic was taken to Elsinore the same year (see Note No. 55).
See also Nos. 216 and 243.

128 This production at Stratford was previously seen there in 1937 with Donald Wolfit as Hamlet (see No. 242). Between 1879 and 1948 Hamlet had been played at the Stratford Memorial Theatre by the following actors:

Barry Sullivan, 1879, 1880.
Frank Benson, 1886, 1888, 1891, 1896, 1898, 1899, 1902 to 1907, 1910 to 1916 (see Note No. 42).
Sarah Bernhardt, 1899 (see Note No. 73).
Matheson Lang, 1908, 1909.
Forbes Robertson, 1908.
Martin Harvey, 1910.
Beerbohm Tree, 1910.
H. B. Irving, 1914, 1916 (in one scene only in a special tercentenary presentation).
William Stack, 1916 (Old Vic Company) and 1922.
Murray Carrington, 1920.
Arthur Phillips, 1924.
John Laurie, 1927.
George Hayes, 1928, 1929, 1930, 1942.
Anew McMaster, 1933.
Donald Wolfit, 1936, 1937 (see No. 242).
Basil Langton, 1940 (see No. 128).
John Byron, 1944 (see No. 134 and No. 220—television).
Paul Scofield and Robert Helpmann (alternating) 1948 (see No. 136).

129 See Note No. 59.

130 This was the first important production of *Hamlet* in the Soviet National Republic of Uzbekistan, which before the Revolution had no theatre of its own. Shakespeare for the first time was translated into the Uzbek language.
See also Nos. 160 and 180.

131 An open-air performance at the Frankfürt Festival 1939, under special patronage of Hitler and Goebbels.

132 An all-negro production. Among other coloured actors, Ira Aldridge, "The African Roscius" included Hamlet in his repertoire in his European tours in the mid-nineteenth century.

133 Maurice Evans first played Hamlet at the Old Vic, 1935 (see Note No. 19). He equalled John Gielgud's record in New York of 132 performances in 1938, when the play was said to have been given in its entirety for the first time in New York. He again played Hamlet in 1939 and 1945. The latter production was known as the "G.I. Hamlet", having been cut and produced for presentation to Army audiences by Maurice Evans during the war. Its costumes were of a timeless period, based on nineteenth-century details. It ran 131 performances in New York, one short of the Gielgud and Evans record.

134 Produced by Robert Atkins on a replica of an Elizabethan stage (see Note No. 128).

135 See Note No. 100.

136 This production was set in the Early Victorian period. Paul Scofield played Hamlet first and alternated with Robert Helpmann throughout the season. Claire Bloom also played Ophelia at the Old Vic 1954 (see page 153).
See also No. 224.

101 London, an early eighteenth-century production (probably Theatre Royal, Drury Lane. Hamlet: Robert Wilkes).

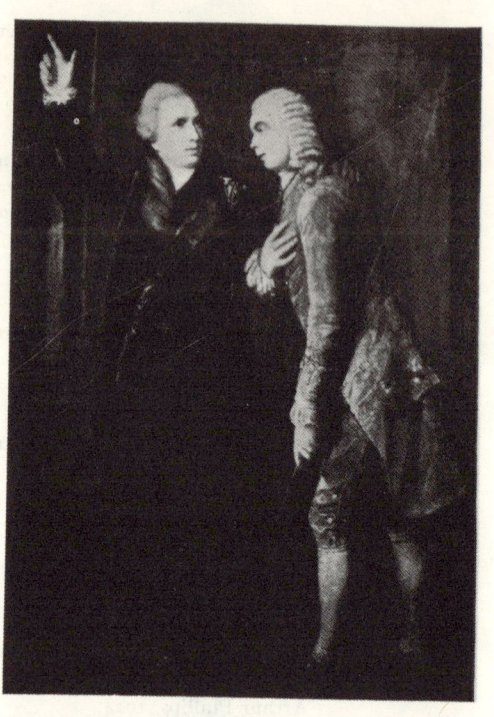

101A London, Covent Garden, 1779. Hamlet: John Henderson; Polonius: Richard Wilson. From a painting by an unknown artist in the W. Somerset Maugham Collection, the property of the National Theatre Trustees.

102 Germany, Berlin, 1778. Hamlet: Johann Brockmann. Ophelia: Caroline Döbbelin. Gertrude: Hancke. Claudius: Johannes Brückner. Produced by Karl Döbbelin.

ACT III SCENE 2

103 Juvenile Drama Set, published by Hodgson, London, between 1822–1830.

104 London, Covent Garden Theatre, 1838. Hamlet: William Charles Macready. Claudius: Charles Diddear. Gertrude: Mary Warner (Miss Huddart). Ophelia: Elizabeth Rainforth. Player King: Mr. Waldron. Produced by William Charles Macready.

105 London, Princess's Theatre, 1850. Set drawing by H. Cuthbert from a design by Thomas Grieve, for Charles Kean's production.

106 London, Haymarket Theatre, 1892. Hamlet: Beerbohm Tree. Ophelia: Mrs. Tree. Polonius: Henry Kemble. Claudius: F. H. Macklin. Gertrude: Rose Leclercq. Horatio: Arthur Dacre. Produced by Beerbohm Tree, settings by William Telbin, Jnr., costumes by Karl.

ACT III SCENE 2

107 London, Theatre Royal, Drury Lane, 1913. Hamlet: Forbes Robertson. Ophelia: Gertrude Elliott. Horatio: S. A. Cookson. Gertrude: Adeline Bourne. Claudius: Walter Ringham. Polonius: J. H. Barnes. Produced by Forbes Robertson, settings by Hawes Craven, costumes by Karl.

108 London, Lyric Theatre, 1905. Hamlet: Martin Harvey. Ophelia: N. de Silva. Gertrude: Maud Milton. Claudius: Charles Glenny. Player King: Charles J. Cameron. Lucianus: L. Arthur. Horatio: Percy Anstey. Polonius: Fred Wright, Snr. Produced by Martin Harvey, settings by George J. Dodson.

109 Japan, Tokio, 1891. Hamlet: Ajiro Fujisawa. Ophelia: Sada Yacco. Produced by Oto Kawakami.

110 Russia, Moscow, Art Theatre, 1911. (Hamlet: Vassily Katchaloff.) The three Players: A. M. Zhelinsky, R. V. Boleslavsky, V. V. Soloveyva. Produced by Stanislavsky, settings and costumes by E. Gordon Craig.

ACT III SCENE 2

111 Germany, Berlin, Deutsches Theater, 1909. Hamlet: Alexander Moissi. Claudius: Paul Wegener. Gertrude: Rosa Bertens. Ophelia: Camilla Eibenschütz. Produced by Max Reinhardt, settings by Ernst Stern.

112 London, Covent Garden Theatre, 1919. Hamlet: Martin Harvey. Gertrude: Miriam Lewes. Claudius: Frederick Ross. Polonius: H. O. Nicholson. Horatio: A. B. Imerson. Produced by Martin Harvey; production designed by Martin Harvey.

113 London, Kingsway Theatre (Barry Jackson's Birmingham Repertory Company), 1925. Hamlet: Colin Keith-Johnston. Polonius: A. Bromley-Davenport. Gertrude: Dorothy Massingham. Claudius: Frank Vosper. Horatio: Alan Howland. Ophelia: Muriel Hewitt. Prologue: Elana Aherne. Produced by H. K. Ayliff, settings and costumes by Paul Shelving.

114 London, Kingsway Theatre (Barry Jackson's Birmingham Repertory Company), 1925. Hamlet: Colin Keith-Johnston. Gertrude: Dorothy Massingham. Horatio: Alan Howland. Player King: Terence O'Brien. Claudius: Frank Vosper. Ophelia: Muriel Hewitt. Player Queen: Norma Varden. Polonius: A. Bromley-Davenport. Produced by H. K. Ayliff, settings and costumes by Paul Shelving.

ACT III SCENE 2

115 London, Haymarket Theatre, 1925. Hamlet: John Barrymore. Gertrude: Constance Collier. Polonius: Herbert Waring. Claudius: Malcolm Keen. Ophelia: Fay Compton. Horatio: George Relph. Produced by John Barrymore, settings by Robert Edmond Jones.

116 U.S.S.R., Moscow, Art Theatre (the 2nd), 1924. (Hamlet: Michael Chekov.) Produced by Michael Chekov, set design by M. V. Libakov.

117 Germany, Berlin, State Theatre, 1927. Hamlet: Fritz Kortner. First Player: Arthur Krausneck. Produced by Leopold Jessner, settings and costumes by Caspar Neher.

118 Germany, Berlin, State Theatre, 1927. (Hamlet: Fritz Kortner.) Claudius: Wäscher. Gertrude: Maria Koppenhöfer. Produced by Leopold Jessner, settings and costumes by Caspar Neher.

ACT III SCENE 2

119 Czechoslovakia, Prague, National Theatre, 1926. Set design by Vlastial Hofman.

120 U.S.S.R., Georgia, Tbilisi (Tiflis), Rustavelli Theatre, 1925. Produced by Madjanushvili.

121 Czechoslovakia, Prague, Municipal Theatre, 1927. Hamlet: Zdenek Stepanek. Produced by Yaroslav Kvapil, settings by Josef Wenig.

122 Czechoslovakia, Prague, Municipal Theatre, 1927. Hamlet: Zdenek Stepanek. Produced by Yaroslav Kvapil, settings by Josef Wenig.

ACT III SCENE 2

123 London, Haymarket Theatre, 1930 (two special matinées). Hamlet: Henry Ainley. Claudius: Malcolm Keen. Gertrude: Irene Vanbrugh. Horatio: Godfrey Tearle. Ophelia: Gwen Ffrangcon-Davies. Polonius: Herbert Waring. Produced by Forbes Robertson, settings by Aubrey Hammond, costumes by Percy Macquoid.

124 London, Old Vic, 1932. Hamlet: Robert Harris. Gertrude: Martita Hunt. Claudius: Alastair Sim. Polonius: Douglas Jeffries. Horatio: Ralph Michael. Lucianus: Harold Chapin. Player King: Frank Napier. Produced by Harcourt Williams, settings and costumes by Owen P. Smyth.

125 London, New Theatre, 1934. Hamlet: John Gielgud. Claudius: Frank Vosper. Ophelia: Jessica Tandy. Horatio: Jack Hawkins. Gertrude: Laura Cowie. Player King: George Devine. Player Queen: Sam Beazley. Lucianus: Alec Guinness. Produced by John Gielgud, settings and costumes by Motley.

126 America, New York, Empire Theatre, 1936. Hamlet: John Gielgud. Claudius: Malcolm Keen. Gertrude: Judith Anderson. Ophelia: Lillian Gish. Horatio: Harry Andrews. Polonius: Anthony Byron. Player King: Harry Mestayer. Player Queen: Ruth March. Produced by Guthrie McClintic, settings and costumes by Jo. Mielziner.

ACT III SCENE 2

127 London, Old Vic, 1937. Hamlet: Laurence Olivier. Ophelia: Cherry Cottrell. Claudius: Francis L. Sullivan. Gertrude: Dorothy Dix. Polonius: George Howe. Horatio: Robert Newton. Player King: Marius Goring. Player Queen: Stuart Burge. Produced by Tyrone Guthrie, settings by Martin Battersby, costumes by Osborne Robinson.

128 England, Stratford-upon-Avon, Memorial Theatre, 1940. Hamlet: Basil Langton. Horatio: Donald Lane-Smith. Ophelia: Peggy Bryan. Polonius: Andrew Leigh. Gertrude: Clare Harris. Claudius: George Skillan. Player King: Stanley Howlett. Lucianus: George Wood. Produced by Iden Payne, settings by Randle Ayrton, costumes by Barbara Curtis.

129 England, Cambridge, Marlowe Society (University Dramatic Society), 1936. Anonymous cast. Produced by George Rylands, settings and costumes by Geoffrey Wright.

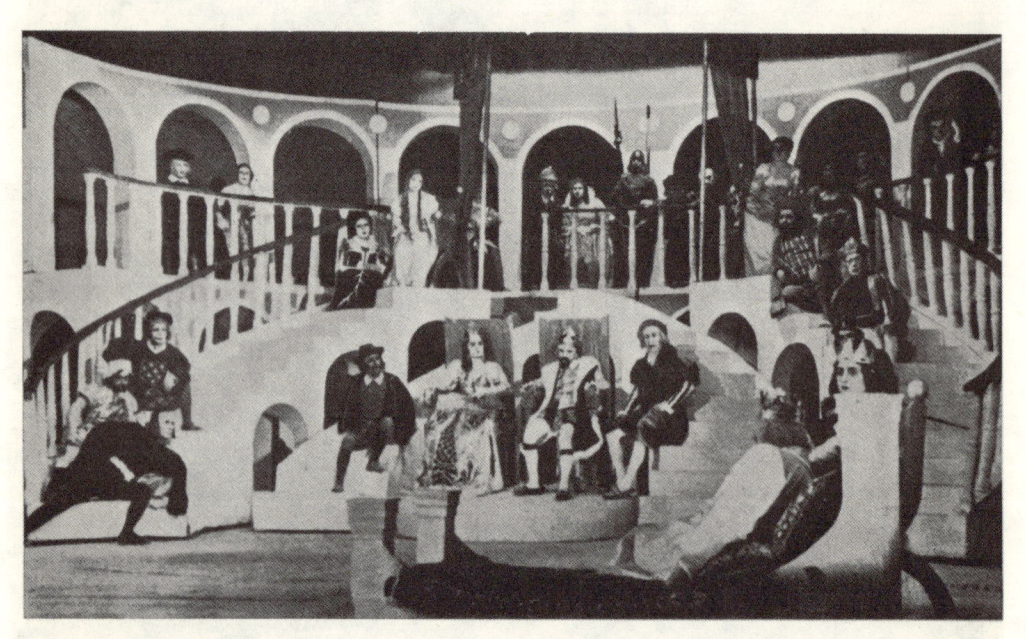

130 U.S.S.R., Uzbekistan, Tashkent, Uzbek State Theatre (called Khamz), 1935. Hamlet: Hidoyatov. Produced by M. Uigur and Babakhodjayev, settings by I. Y. Shlepyanov.

ACT III SCENE 2

131 Germany, Frankfurt Festival, 1939. Hamlet: Wolfgang Büttner. Claudius: Walter Richter. Gertrude: Ellen Daub. Ophelia: Else Knott. Produced by Hans Meissner, setting and costumes by Caspar Neher.

132 America, New York, Hampton Institute, 1945. Hamlet: Gordon Heath. Gertrude: Dorothy Adeca. Claudius: Owen Dobson. Ophelia: Marion Douglas. Polonius: Austin Brigg-Hall. Produced by Oliver Dobson, settings and costumes by Charles Sebree.

133 America, New York, St. James's Theatre, 1938. Hamlet: Maurice Evans. Ophelia: Katherine Locke. Claudius: Henry Edwards. Gertrude: Mady Christians. Polonius: George Graham. Player King: Rhys Williams. Player Queen: Paul Nevens. Produced by Margaret Webster, settings and costumes by David Ffolkes.

134 England, Stratford-upon-Avon, Memorial Theatre, 1944. Hamlet: John Byron. Gertrude: Viola Lyel. Horatio: David Reid. Claudius: Raymond Rollett. Ophelia: Anna Burden. Polonius: Michael Martin-Harvey. Player King: Clement Hamlin. Lucianus: Lionel Blair. Produced by Robert Atkins, setting by Guy Sheppard, costumes by Barbara Curtis.

ACT III SCENE 2

135 England, Bristol, Theatre Royal (Old Vic Company), 1948. Hamlet: Robert Eddison. Gertrude: Catherine Lacey. Claudius: Alexander Gauge. Polonius: Paul Rogers. Ophelia: Jane Wenham. Player King: John Glen. Player Queen: Christopher Page. Lucianus: Henry Manning. Horatio: Rolf Lefebvre. Produced by Hugh Hunt, settings and costumes by Alan Barlow.

136 England, Stratford-upon-Avon, Memorial Theatre, 1948. Hamlet: Paul Scofield (alternating with Robert Helpmann). Claudius: Anthony Quayle. Gertrude: Diana Wynyard. Ophelia: Claire Bloom. Horatio: John Justin. Polonius: John Kidd. Player King: Michael Godfrey. Player Queen: Ailsa Grahame. Produced by Michael Benthall, settings and costumes by James Bailey.

Act III Scene 3

A ROOM IN THE CASTLE

(*The King's Closet*)

Directly after the performance the King has given Rosencrantz and Guildenstern the commission long since decided on, of accompanying Hamlet immediately to England; a commission that they accept all too readily. Yet he now gives himself up to pious thoughts and heart-searching meditations, such as are suited to the hour of evening prayer. The King is no hardened sinner. On the contrary, he is well aware of the heinous nature of his crime, though he knows that he cannot pray heaven for mercy as long as he enjoys the fruits of his evil-doing, and does not doubt that the day will come when judgment will be meted out to him; but he clings too obstinately to what he holds for any genuine repentance. At this moment when he is on his knees in prayer Hamlet appears behind him on his way to his mother's room.

But Hamlet does not strike because he finds his victim in prayer. True revenge can indeed only be taken according to the formula: an eye for an eye, a tooth for a tooth. Only thus would he satisfy the Ghost, whose bitter complaint still seems to be ringing in Hamlet's ears, the complaint that as the old King had been sent unprepared and 'unhouseled' to his death his spirit must now endure all the torments of purgatory. To send this murderer, therefore, to his death at a moment so propitious for the welfare of his soul is not punishment enough. Thus he allows his one and only opportunity of accomplishing his bloody task to escape him. A moment later the King rises from his knees unconscious of how near he has been to death.

NOTES:

137   See Note No. 2.   138   See Note No. 51.   139   See Note No. 53.
140   See Note No. 18. An interesting piece of business was introduced in this production. Hamlet did not wear a sword in the Play scene, but one was carried before the King. In the Closet scene following he removed his crown but kept the sword beside him. It was this sword that Hamlet picked up, intending to kill Claudius, and retained in his hand into the following scene, using it to kill Polonius. The King's finishing his prayer and noticing the loss of his sword made a climax to the scene.
141   See Note No. 58.
142   See Note No. 10.
        Basil Sydney also played Claudius in the Old Vic Company production at the New Theatre, 1944 (see Note No. 25). He played Hamlet in a modern dress production, New York, 1925.
142A An interesting modern dress production was given by the Bromley Repertory Company. It included many startling effects and innovations. "The King's Closet scene," the producer Geoffrey Edwards says "was set on a terrace looking into the King's chamber through French windows. The King came out on to the terrace for his scene with Polonius, Rosencrantz and Guildenstern and his soliloquy; he then retired into his room to pray, and was visible through the windows, kneeling inside. Hamlet enters, walking along the terrace towards his Mother's bedroom, and sees the kneeling figure of the King through the window. Instantly he stops and draws from his pocket the gun which has been given him significantly by Horatio at the end of the Play Scene—aiming it through the window at the King he speaks the lines beginning: ' Now might I do it

[*continued on opposite page.*

ACT III SCENE 3

137 London, Princess's Theatre, 1850. Set drawing by H. Cuthbert from a design by Thomas Grieve for Charles Kean's production.

138 Holland, Amsterdam, Municipal Theatre, 1918. Design by H. th. Wijdeveld.

NOTE : continued.

142A
pat . . .' thereby, in my opinion, overcoming successfully for the first time, the uncomfortable feeling the audience has in most productions of *Hamlet* of wondering why the King does not (as it were) overhear Hamlet's soliloquy. Hamlet then proceeds along the terrace to his Mother's bedroom, and the King rises from his attempt at prayer, opens the French windows and speaks the concluding lines of the scene."

139 Czechoslovakia, Prague, National Theatre, 1926. Set design by Vlastial Hofman.

140 London, New Theatre, 1934. Hamlet: John Gielgud. Claudius: Frank Vosper. Produced by John Gielgud, settings and costumes by Motley.

ACT III SCENE 3

141 Poland, Warsaw, Polski Theatre, 1947. Hamlet: Marian Wyrzkowski. Produced by Arnold Szyffman, settings by Karol Frycz.

142 England, Two Cities Film for the J. Arthur Rank Organization, 1948. Hamlet: Laurence Olivier. Claudius: Basil Sydney. Directed by Laurence Olivier, settings and costumes by Roger Furse.

142A England, Bromley, New Theatre, 1952. Hamlet: John Bennett. Claudius: John Carew. Produced by Geoffrey Edwards, settings and costumes by John Burnand.

Act III Scene 4

THE QUEEN'S CLOSET

THE moment has come at last when Hamlet can unburden himself to the Queen of all the rancour that has poisoned his thoughts for months. In his bitterness of spirit he receives her words of censure rudely. And when, surprised and indignant, she shows that her maternal dignity is affronted and makes as though to leave the room, with a veiled threat to send others to him, he rushes at her in fury, and roughly thrusts her into a chair; so that in sudden fear she gives the cry for help that costs Polonius his life when he responds to it. For Hamlet suddenly plunges his sword through the arras with a mocking cry of triumph, and an ironical boast about the sureness of his aim, as though he were merely indulging in the sport of killing vermin. The deed is done, as his reply to the horrified Queen shows, without his having any clear idea of the identity of the eavesdropper. A moment later it occurs to him that his victim may be the King himself. He finds at once that this is not so, but from now on he seems impervious to all else, it is virtually of no account to him whom he has killed, for he once more turns to his horrified mother, who attempts in vain to make him realize the terrible nature of what he has done. An important point is cleared up here by his defiant rejoinder hinting that she too was implicated in the murder of the old King. Queen Gertrude, in fact, knows nothing of this crime. But now she is deeply shaken morally. It is at this moment that Hamlet plunges into a description of her erotic pleasures.

At this moment, however, the Ghost once again appears to the avenger. This sudden visitation momentarily stems the torrent of Hamlet's wrath. He stares at it aghast, for its return must surely mean that he has been remiss in his duty. But the Ghost is not simply concerned with revenge; it has come to pacify Hamlet and to counsel him to be gentle towards his mother. Hamlet makes no answer. His heart contracts at its pitiful aspect, and he feels his strength ebbing away in deep-felt sympathy and compassion.

The Queen, who cannot see the apparition, thinks he must be out of his mind, but Hamlet hastily reassures her, anxious to leave to her no excuse for treating what he has said as the vapouring of a madman. He again becomes calm enough to demonstrate to her that he has been speaking with all his wits about him. And so he goes on with his lenten sermon.

At the end of this interview it becomes clear that Hamlet already knows of the commission that is to take him to England. He suspects, too rightly, that the plan conceals a dangerous plot directed against himself. The risk of danger arouses in him a fierce joy in the contest, for he begins to see his enemies falling into the trap they intend to set for him. After this glimpse into the obscurity of the future he finally takes leave of his mother and drags away with him the body of Polonius, with a heartless jest.

ACT III SCENE 4

NOTES:

143　The first illustrated edition of Shakespeare was that edited by Nicholas Rowe and published by Jacob Tonson in 1709. There is a frontispiece to each play, and many are undoubtedly drawings from contemporary stage productions. The plates were re-engraved in a smaller size for Theobald's edition of 1734. The first imaginative attempt to illustrate Shakespeare was made by Francis Hayman for Sir Thomas Hanner's edition, Oxford 1743-4. At the time of the 1709 edition Thomas Betterton was the most famous Hamlet. He first played the character at the Lincoln's Inn Theatre, December 1661; his wife, Mary Saunderson, was Ophelia. This was the first production after the introduction of women actresses to the public stage in December 1660. Betterton last played Hamlet at Drury Lane in 1709. He was seventy-five years old (see Note No. 183). *Hamlet* was first performed (in the Folio version, see Note No. 183) at the Globe, Bankside, in 1601-2 with Richard Burbage as Hamlet when tradition ascribed the part of the Ghost to Shakespeare himself.

144　This picture at one time was thought to represent Betterton and Mrs. Barry (the earlier), but the costume suggests a date *c.* 1748, which makes this impossible. It is almost certainly the work of Francis Hayman. There is no authentic portrait of Mrs. Elmy, who is now thought to be the Gertrude, but the Hamlet is very like the other portrait of Spranger Barry (see following Note). Barry first played Hamlet at Drury Lane in 1747. It is not known who played the Queen and the Ghost.

　　An engraving from this picture was published as a frontispiece to an edition of the play in 1773. The artist is given as Hayman, but the costumes have been brought up to contemporary date.

145　This is an authentic portrait of Spranger Barry and his wife Ann. The likeness to the picture painted some twenty-five years earlier is unmistakable. It is interesting to note the business of the overturned chair in all three of these early Closet scenes. Many writers have credited this business to Garrick but its origin is obviously of an earlier date. Henderson in 1777 was brought to task by the critics for omitting what was called " the established custom ". In repeating this, John Ireland in *The Letters and Poems of John Henderson* comments: " The chair in which Mr. Garrick sat, when he played in the Closet Scene, was somewhat different from that appropriated to the Queen, the cabriol feet being tapered, and placed so much under the seat, that it fell with a touch ". This undoubtedly happened at the moment of the Ghost's appearance.

146　See Note No. 102.

147　See Note No. 67.

148　John Philip Kemble first played Hamlet at Covent Garden in 1783, and continued to play the part until his retirement in 1817. He founded a school of acting which lasted well into the nineteenth century. He broke the ' modern dress ' tradition and wore a costume which was a stage adaptation of the Elizabethan style which remained in vogue till 1838 when Charles Kean introduced the tunic, still with Elizabethan trimmings, but these gradually vanished and the more severe costume was evolved.

　　In France Talma was responsible for the reformation of stage costume at the same period; he played Hamlet dressed as a German student of the sixteenth century; like Kemble, he also introduced correct Roman togas for classical plays. He appeared in London in 1817.

　　See also No. 195.

149　See Note No. 30.

150　Phelps first played Hamlet in London at the Haymarket, 1837. During his seasons at Sadler's Wells, 1844 to 1861, he played the part many times, the first being in 1847. He revived all the plays of Shakespeare excepting *Henry VI, Troilus and Cressida, Titus Andronicus* and *Richard II*—a record he held until 1923 when the Old Vic became the first theatre in the world to have produced all the plays included in the First Folio (with the addition of *Pericles*).

151 See Note No. 2.

152 See Note No. 3.

153 See Note No. 107.

154 See Note No. 15.

155 See Note No. 50.

156 This production made interesting use of a permanent false proscenium with changes of backcloth.
   See also No. 172.

157 See Note No. 9.

158 See Note No. 7.

159 See Note No. 58.

160 See Note No. 130.

161 See Note No. 113.

162 Akimov did not hesitate to replace, rewrite and even add new scenes to the play to force it to his conception of being simply Hamlet's fight for his throne. This bedroom scene between Claudius and Gertrude was one of these interpolated scenes.
   See also Nos. 215 and 241.

163 Polonius was stabbed through a courtly figure woven in the arras behind which he was hiding.

164 See Note No. 121.

165 See Note No. 25.

166 See Note No. 10.

Germany, Bochum, Park Theatre, 1952. Hamlet: Hans Messemer. Set design by Max Fritzsche.

This production by Hans Schalla at the Shakespeare Festival, Bochum, April 1952, on the occasion of the annual general meeting of the German Shakespeare Society, used a text based on the translation by Johann Joachim Eichenberg published between 1774 and 1782. (See also page 152 for the setting in use.)

ACT III SCENE 4

143 The frontispiece to the first illustrated edition of the play. Edited by Nicholas Rowe, 1709. (Published by Jacob Tonson.)

144 London, Theatre Royal, Drury Lane, 1747. Hamlet: Spranger Barry. Gertrude: Mrs. Elmy? From a painting by Francis Hayman, c. 1748, in the Garrick Club.

145 London, Theatre Royal, Drury Lane, 1778. Hamlet: Spranger Barry. Gertrude: Mrs. Ann Barry. From a painting by James Roberts in the Garrick Club.

146 Germany, Berlin, 1778. Hamlet: Johann Brockmann. Ghost: Karl Döbbelin. Gertrude: Hancke. Produced by Karl Döbbelin.

147 London, Haymarket Theatre, 1777. Hamlet: John Henderson. From a painting by Robert Dunkerton in the National Portrait Gallery.

148 London, Covent Garden Theatre, 1783. Hamlet: John Philip Kemble.

149 London, Princess's Theatre, 1845. Hamlet: William Charles Macready. Gertrude: Frances Ternan. Produced by William Charles Macready, settings by William Beverley and Mr. Nicholls.

150 London, Sadler's Wells Theatre, 1847. Hamlet: Samuel Phelps. Gertrude: Isabella Glyn. Produced by Samuel Phelps, settings by Messrs. Fenton and Finlay.

ACT III SCENE 4

151 London, Princess's Theatre, 1850. Set drawing by I. Day from a design by Thomas Grieve, for Charles Kean's production.

152 London, Lyceum Theatre, 1864. (Hamlet: Charles Fechter.) Set design by William Telbin, Snr.

153 London, Lyceum Theatre, 1897, Hamlet: Forbes Robertson. Ghost: Ian Robertson. Gertrude: Charlotte Granville. Produced by Forbes Robertson, settings by Hawes Craven, costumes by Karl.

154 Germany, Mannheim, Court Theatre, 1907. Set design by Dr. Carl Hagemann.

ACT III SCENE 4

155 Germany, Berlin, Deutsches Theater, 1908. Hamlet: Alexander Moissi. Gertrude: Rosa Bertens. Ghost: Wilhelm Diegelmann. Produced by Max Reinhardt, settings by Ernst Stern.

156 Germany, Munich, Court Theatre, 1913. Produced by Caesar Klein, settings by Eugen Kilian.

157 France, Film, Lux Company, 1910. Hamlet: Jacques Grétillat. Gertrude: Colonna Romano. Directed by Henri Deffontaines.

158 America, New York, Hampden's Theatre, 1925. (Hamlet: Walter Hampden.) Set design by Claude Bragdon.

ACT III SCENE 4

159 Poland, Warsaw, Polski Theatre, 1947. Hamlet: Marian Wryzykowski. Produced by Arnold Szyffman, settings by Karol Frycz.

160 U.S.S.R., Uzbekistan, Tashkent, Uzbek State Theatre (called Khamz), 1935. Hamlet: Hidoyatov. Produced by M. Uigur and Babakhodjayev, settings by I. Y. Shlepyanov.

161 London, Kingsway Theatre (Barry Jackson's Birmingham Repertory Company), 1925. Hamlet: Colin Keith-Johnston. Gertrude: Dorothy Massingham. Polonius: A. Bromley-Davenport. Produced by H. K. Ayliff, settings and costumes by Paul Shelving.

162 U.S.S.R., Moscow, Vahtangov Theatre, 1931. (Hamlet: Gorunov.) Claudius: Rubin Simonov. Production and settings by Nicolai Akimov.

163 U.S.S.R., Moscow, Vahtangov Theatre, 1931. Hamlet: Gorunov. Production and settings by Nicolai Akimov.

ACT III SCENE 4
103

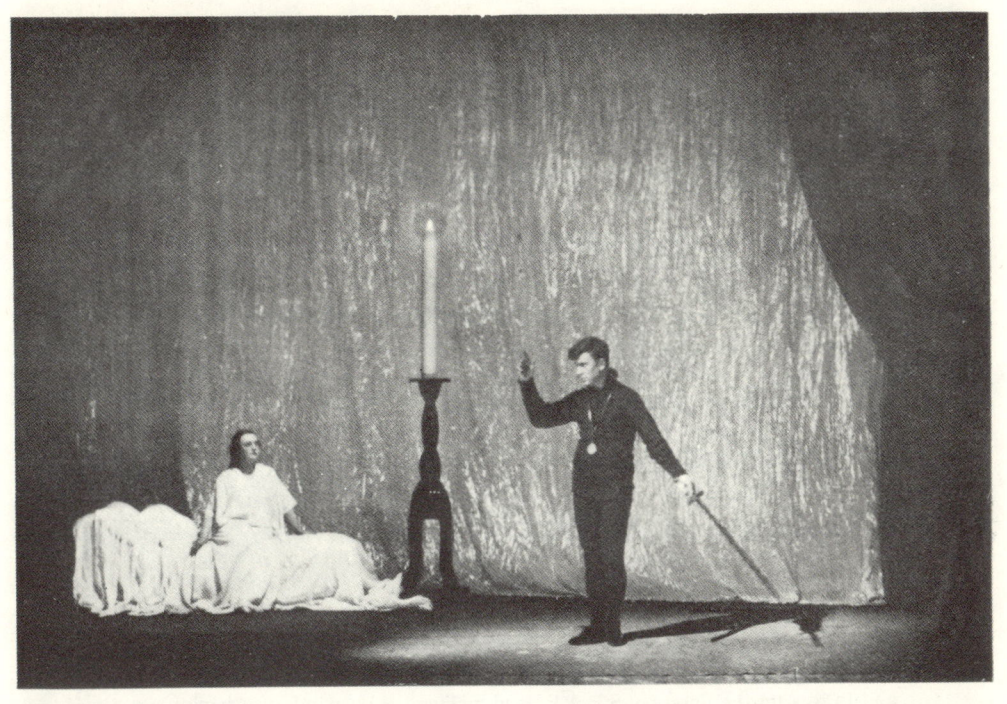

164 Czechoslovakia, Prague, Municipal Theatre, 1927. Hamlet: Zdenek Stepanek. Produced by Yaroslav Kvapil, settings by Josef Wenig.

165 London, New Theatre, Old Vic Company, 1944. Hamlet: Robert Helpmann. Gertrude: Margot Grahame. Produced by Tyrone Guthrie and Michael Benthall, settings and costumes by Leslie Hurry.

166 England, Two Cities Film for the J. Arthur Rank Organization, 1948. Hamlet: Laurence Olivier. Gertrude: Eileen Herlie. Directed by Laurence Olivier, settings and costumes by Roger Furse.

Act IV Scene 1

A ROOM IN THE CASTLE

(*Usually played as a return to the King's Closet*)

THE action of this scene follows immediately upon the preceding one. Day has not yet dawned. The King enters the Queen's room, finding her in the state of collapse in which Hamlet had left her and asks the reason for her affliction. She then recounts the events of the night. In doing so she attempts, where possible, to shield her son, dwelling on his abnormal condition. The King listens to her without expressing any sympathy for Polonius. He decides to delay no longer in sending Hamlet to England. The first and most important thing for him to do now is to discover where Hamlet has hidden the body of Polonius. Rosencrantz and Guildenstern undertake to extract the information.

NOTES:

167 See Note No. 1.
168 John Gielgud's third London *Hamlet* produced in a season of repertory at the Haymarket Theatre 1944–5. Following the season John Gielgud took a company on a tour of India and Burma for the Forces of S.E.A.C., and included *Hamlet* in his repertoire.
See also No. 222 and Note No. 18.

Charles Kean as Hamlet. From a painting by William Daniels in the Victoria and Albert Museum, London. This picture shows Kean in the tunic costume which he introduced. It was probably painted at Liverpool in 1838. (See Note No. 70 and page 27.)

ACT IV SCENE 1

167 Juvenile Drama Scene, published by West, London, 1815. Backcloth and wing.

Edwin Booth as Hamlet. Princess's Theatre, London, 1880. (See Note No. 7.) It is interesting to note that the Ophelia of this production, Florence Gerard, wore in the mad scene, what appears from a photograph to have been a black dress, most certainly it was of a dark material. (See Note No. 181.)

168 London, Haymarket Theatre, 1944. (Hamlet: John Gielgud.) Claudius: Leslie Banks. Gertrude: Marian Spencer. Produced by George Rylands, settings by Ruth Keating, costumes by Jeanetta Cochrane.

Act IV Scene 2

ANOTHER ROOM IN THE CASTLE

(This and the following scenes are usually combined in the acting versions and severely cut)

ROSENCRANTZ and Guildenstern fail in their attempt to discover where Hamlet has hidden the body of Polonius; they are no more successful than they were when trying to sound Hamlet on a former occasion.

NOTE:

169   See Note No. 1.

Act IV Scene 3

ANOTHER ROOM IN THE CASTLE

ROSENCRANTZ and Guildenstern leave it to the King to question Hamlet and by perseverance he succeeds in getting a hint from him that leads to the finding of the body beneath the stairs.

This ignominious contest over the remains of Polonius shows a definite deterioration in Hamlet's mental condition. After Hamlet has gone the soliloquy spoken by the King shows that he expects to recover the peace he has so completely lost only by the death of Hamlet. He will arrange for Hamlet to be sent to England at once, accompanied by Rosencrantz and Guildenstern with letters requiring the death of Hamlet immediately on his arrival.

NOTE:

170   It was announced at the time of this production that this scene was being played for the first time in London. It was set in the Hall of the Castle (See Note No. 43).

ACT IV SCENES 2 AND 3

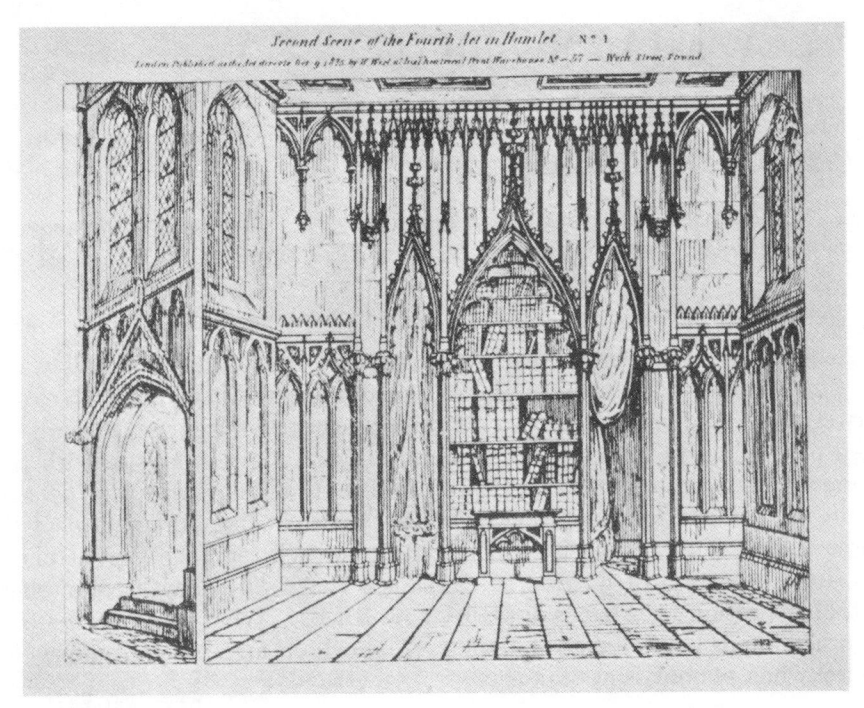

169 Juvenile Drama Scene, published by West, London, 1815. Backcloth and wing.

170 London, Lyceum Theatre, 1909. Hamlet: Matheson Lang. Claudius: Eric Mayne. Rosencrantz: Sydney Vautier. Guildenstern: Cowley Wright. Produced by Ernest Carpenter, settings by E. C. Nicholls.

Act IV Scene 4

A PLAIN IN DENMARK

(This scene was usually cut in the acting versions until recent years. It was first replaced by John Gielgud at the New Theatre in 1934)

Hamlet sets forth to take ship for England, but on his way he has one last encounter of a certain importance. The forces of the Norwegian, Fortinbras, about to conduct a campaign against Poland, have asked permission to march through Denmark and Hamlet falls in with them. He inquires the reason for the war and is told that honour is the principal cause, for the objects of the quarrel, on which so much is being staked, are of little consequence. This gives him much matter for self-reproach, for at once he compares the action of Fortinbras with his own. Is he deluding himself into mistaking caution for what is in reality cowardice? What an object lesson, on the other hand, is offered by Fortinbras, for whom any pretext suffices for a quarrel when honour is at stake.

NOTES:

171   This design by Svend Gade, a Danish artist, who in 1920 directed the Asta Nielsen film of *Hamlet* (see No. 97), was for a production with Joseph Kainz as Hamlet. See also No. 200.

172   See Note No. 156.

173   See Note No. 121.

174   See Note No. 8. An interesting setting for this scene was designed by Stewart Chaney for Leslie Howard's Hamlet in New York in 1936, when it was set on board a Viking ship. Howard himself was the producer.

ACT IV SCENE 4

171 Germany, Berlin, Neues Schauspielhaus, 1909. (Hamlet: Joseph Kainz.) Set design by Svend Gade.

172 Germany, Munich, Court Theatre, 1913. Produced by Caesar Klein, settings by Eugen Kilian.

173 Czechoslovakia, Prague, Municipal Theatre, 1927. Hamlet : Zdenek Stepanek. Produced by Yaroslav Kvapil, settings by Josef Wenig.

174 London, Arts Theatre, 1945. (Hamlet : Alec Clunes.) Produced by Judith Furse, settings by Michael Warre.

Act IV Scene 5

A ROOM IN THE CASTLE

(This is usually played in the Hall of the Castle and in some acting versions Scene 7 is played as a continuation of this scene, omitting Scene 6)

WEEKS, perhaps months, have passed since the preceding events. Fortinbras in the meantime has started his homeward march after the victorious campaign against Poland, and Laertes has returned from Paris. The death of Polonius, never explained, and his secret burial, have caused suspicion and discontent among the populace, endangering the position of the King. The Queen's equanimity has given way to a progressive feeling of guilt. Tragedy in fact soon appears in the form of the madness of Ophelia, who makes her way singing into the Castle with wild gestures and disordered hair, in a manner that leaves no doubt of her complete mental derangement. At the instigation of unknown enemies of Claudius, Laertes breaks into the palace, sword in hand, crying aloud for vengeance and already acclaimed as King by his supporters. With passionate vehemence he lays the blame for his father's death upon the King. But Claudius, by his imperturbable behaviour, succeeds in persuading Laertes to restrain himself and discuss things reasonably.

This, however, is jeopardized by the sudden return of Ophelia, singing snatches of lewd songs and scattering flowers, and her pitiable condition again arouses the bitterest feelings in her brother's heart. All the same, once he has listened to the King's explanations, he is utterly deluded by the latter's superior skill in handling men even to the point of becoming his tool. The King stimulates Laertes' hatred of Hamlet so effectively that his one desire is to avenge himself personally on Hamlet.

NOTES:

175 This was Mrs. Lessingham's first appearance on the stage; the Hamlet was William (Gentleman) Smith. This print gives a good idea of the traditional contemporary dressing of the Mad Scene. It retained the same characteristics, whatever period was chosen for the setting of the play, till comparatively modern times (see page 122).

176 Helena Modjeska was a noted Polish actress who came to England and later settled in America. She played Ophelia in English to the Hamlet of Edwin Booth in New York, 1889.

177 Ellen Terry first played Ophelia with Irving at the Lyceum in the revival of 1878. See also Note No. 41.

178 See Note No. 45.

179 Vera Komisarjevskaya, sister of Theodore Komisarjevsky, was one of Russia's greatest actresses. She was a member of the Imperial Theatre till 1902, then till her death in 1910 she managed her own theatre in Petrograd.

180 See Note No. 130.

181 and 182 Mrs. Patrick Campbell was the Ophelia in Forbes Robertson's first production of *Hamlet* in 1897. He introduced for the Mad Scene a note of mourning for Polonius by allowing Ophelia to wear a black veil over her traditional white dress. This was a concession to modern convention; white was the colour of mourning in the seventeenth century. When the play was toured Forbes Robertson's wife, Gertrude Elliott, played the part (1900). She was also in the revivals of 1902 and 1913. For her costume she wore complete black, and was said to be the first Ophelia to do so (see page 94). Ellen

112   HAMLET THROUGH THE AGES

Terry had raised the question of a black dress with Irving, but had been informed that white was the correct colour for mourning and anyway " There *must* be only *one* black figure in this play, and that's Hamlet ! " See also Note No. 107.

183 and 183A William Poel first appeared on the stage in 1876. He managed the Royal Victoria Hall, later the Old Vic, for two years. For ten years he was general instructor to the Shakespeare Reading Society, and founded the Elizabethan Stage Society in 1895. To him we owe the revived interest in the staging of Elizabethan drama in its contemporary manner. One of his earliest productions was *Hamlet* on an Elizabethan stage at St. George's Hall in 1881. He used the First Quarto version, printed in 1603, of which only two copies are known to exist; this is a much shorter play than the Folio version of 1623 (see end-paper). Ophelia in the First Quarto version is called Ofelia. Maud Holt, playing in this production as Helen Maude, became the wife of Beerbohm Tree in 1883. She was a well-known amateur actress at the time, as were the whole of the cast of this production, except William Poel himself, who played Hamlet.

Poel revived the play, among subsequent occasions, at Carpenters Hall, on 21 February, 1900, with boys in the female roles, as in Elizabethan times. This photograph shows one of these latter productions.

Poel also produced, for the first time in England, " Fratricide Punished, or Hamlet Prince of Denmark ", a version of *Hamlet* played by English companies who toured the continent during the seventeenth century. Though it followed the plot, it condensed and simplified the dialogue, introducing much comedy relief and dumb-show, to make the play intelligible to foreign audiences. A manuscript German translation of this lost acting version, dated 1710, was preserved in the Vienna State Library and was eventually re-translated into English and produced by Poel at the Playhouse, Oxford, in 1924. It was also staged at the New Oxford Theatre, London, the same year, with Esmé Percy as Hamlet and Margaret Scudamore as the Queen (called Sigri in the play). They repeated these parts in scenes from this production at the Poel centenary matinée at the Old Vic, 11 July, 1952.

There was an earlier play of *Hamlet*, now lost, attributed to Thomas Kyd, produced at ' The Theatre ' between 1587 and 1589, and revived in 1594. The *Hamlet* known to have been produced at the Curtain Theatre between 1596 and 1598 may have been this version partially rewritten by Shakespeare. His completed play was produced at the Globe 1601–2. It is thought that the incomplete version was pirated during the performance at the Curtain Theatre and printed (the First Quarto). The Second Quarto is twice as long as the First and the Folio version as we know it is still longer.

There are six Quarto versions of the play each mainly derived, with variations, from its predecessor (except for the pirated version of 1603). The dates of the other Quartos are 1604, 1605, 1611, undated and 1637. The Folio of 1623 first divides the play into acts and scenes and is considered to be an acting version of the play.

Other stage productions of the First Quarto include : one at the Arts Theatre with John Wyse as Hamlet in 1929 and another at the Rudolf Steiner Hall by the O.U.D.S. in 1949. This production was dressed in mid-eighteenth-century costume.

Hamlet was staged in the Elizabethan manner by Nugent Monck at the Maddermarket Theatre, Norwich, 1930.

184 See Note No. 108. In this scene N. de Silva wore her hair short. Martin Harvey, the producer, held the idea that because of the fever Ophelia, as was the custom, would have had her hair cut. Another innovation was for the mad girl to place the country flowers in the form of a cross on the ground and, between her snatches of song, pray over them.

This business though new to London had been used by Virginia Harned in E. H. Sothern's production, New York, 1900.

185 The setting of this scene in the open air, in this case an orchard, was used occasionally in nineteenth-century productions. See also Note No. 107.

186 When Scene 7 is played at the end of this scene, in some productions the body of Ophelia is brought on after the Queen's " Willow " speech as a climax to the scene. This was a general practice in the late nineteenth and early twentieth centuries. See also Note No. 43.

    187 See Note No. 18.   189 See Note No. 17.
    188 See Note No. 77.   190 See Note No. 18.
                      191 See Note No. 10.

ACT IV SCENE 5

175 London, Theatre Royal, Drury Lane, 1772. (Hamlet: William Smith.) Ophelia: Mrs. Lessingham.

176 Poland, Warsaw, Imperial Theatre, 1871. (Hamlet: Krolilowski.) Ophelia: Helena Modjeska.

177 London, Lyceum Theatre, 1878. (Hamlet: Henry Irving.) Ophelia: Ellen Terry.

178 Japan, Tokio, 1891. (Hamlet: Ajiro Fujisawa.) Ophelia: Sada Yacco.

179 Russia, Petrograd, Imperial Alexandrissky Theatre, 1901. Ophelia: Vera Komisarjevskaya.

180 U.S.S.R., Uzbekistan, Tashkent, Uzbek State Theatre (called Khamz), 1931. Ophelia: Ishanturayeva.

181 London, Lyceum Theatre, 1897. (Hamlet: Forbes Robertson.) Ophelia: Mrs. Patrick Campbell.

182 London, Lyric Theatre, 1902. (Hamlet: Forbes Robertson.) Ophelia: Gertrude Elliott.

ACT IV SCENE 5

183 London, *c.* 1900. A William Poel production of Hamlet on an Elizabethan stage, with an all male cast.

183A London, St. George's Hall, 1881. (Hamlet: William Poel.) Ophelia: Helen Maude (Maude Holt). Gertrude: Zoe Bland.

184 London, Lyric Theatre, 1905. (Hamlet: Martin Harvey.) Ophelia: N. de Silva.

185 London, Lyceum Theatre, 1897. (Hamlet: Forbes Robertson.) Claudius: H. Cooper Cliffe. Gertrude: Charlotte Granville. Ophelia: Mrs. Patrick Campbell. Laertes: Bernard Gould. Produced by Forbes Robertson, settings by Hawes Craven, costumes by Karl.

186 London, Lyceum Theatre, 1909. (Hamlet: Matheson Lang.) Gertrude: Mary Allestree, Claudius: Eric Mayne. Ophelia: Hutin Britton. Laertes: Lauderdale Maitland. Produced by Ernest Carpenter, settings by E. C. Nicholls.

ACT IV SCENE 5

187 London, New Theatre, 1934. (Hamlet: John Gielgud.) Claudius: Frank Vosper. Gertrude: Laura Cowie. Laertes: Glen Byam Shaw. Ophelia: Jessica Tandy. Produced by John Gielgud, settings and costumes by Motley.

188 Germany, Dresden, State Theatre, 1927. (Hamlet: Steinböck.) Horatio: Paulsen. Ophelia: Dietrich. Gertrude: Volckmar. Claudius: Willy Kleinoschegg. Produced by Gerhart Hauptmann, settings by Adolf Mahnke.

189 London, Haymarket Theatre, 1925. (Hamlet: John Barrymore.) Claudius: Malcolm Keen. Gertrude: Constance Collier. Ophelia: Fay Compton. Laertes: Ian Fleming. Produced by John Barrymore, settings by Robert Edmond Jones.

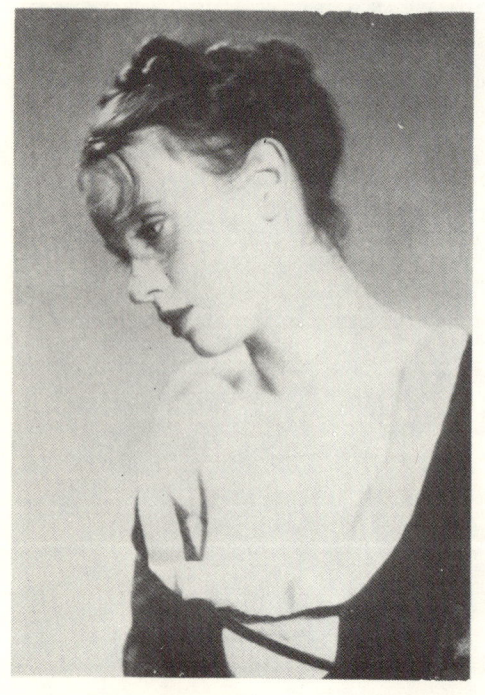

190 London, New Theatre, 1934. (Hamlet: John Gielgud.) Ophelia: Jessica Tandy.

191 England, Two Cities Film for the J. Arthur Rank Organization, 1948. (Hamlet: Laurence Olivier.) Ophelia: Jean Simmons. Laertes: Terence Morgan. Directed by Laurence Olivier, settings and costumes by Roger Furse.

Act IV Scene 6

ANOTHER ROOM IN THE CASTLE

HAMLET is supposed to be on his way to England, but at this moment news comes that owing to a curious chain of circumstances he has returned to Denmark.

It is to Horatio that a sailor brings a letter from Hamlet telling how while on the way to England their ship was waylaid by pirates and how he had managed to be taken prisoner by them in the fight—leaving Rosencrantz and Guildenstern to continue on their way to England. Horatio leaves to join his friend.

Act IV Scene 7

ANOTHER ROOM IN THE CASTLE

(This scene in some acting versions is played as a continuation of Scene 5)

THE King learns of the unexpected return of Hamlet. Laertes succumbs to the flattery and guile of the King, agreeing to a plan for disposing of Hamlet by means of an apparently innocent bout with the foils, in which he will make use of an unbated weapon, and offers to poison it so that there can be no escape for the victim. The King puts the crowning touch to the plan by announcing that he will have a cup of poison ready for Hamlet. This criminal plot has hardly been hatched when the Queen brings the tragic news of Ophelia's death. The demented girl has been wandering by a stream trying to hang her garlands upon the willows; losing her footing she has fallen into the water, and making no effort to save herself has drowned. Laertes, a moment ago consumed by anger, is now benumbed by grief. Twice he asks for confirmation that she has really lost her life and then hastens away, ashamed of the tears he cannot hide.

On the further course of the action Ophelia's madness has only this effect that by it Laertes' desire for vengeance, already strong enough, is yet increased.

Act V Scene 1

A CHURCHYARD

THE first scene of the last act is laid in a churchyard where a grave digger and his assistant are discovered at work. From their conversation it appears that a grave is being prepared for one who has taken her own life, and this leads to various comic and witty observations. When the first grave digger has sent the other away and is alone singing at his work Hamlet and Horatio come into the graveyard, led there apparently by chance. Hamlet's sensitive feelings are shocked by the callousness of a grave digger who can sing at so grim a task, and treat the skulls of men with such indifference. This leads him to ponder all the more on the lot of these men during life. For further information he turns again to the grave digger, who, with his ready mother wit, takes great delight in confounding his interlocutor. A kind of duel of wits develops between them, in which the grave digger, comically enough, gets the better of the Prince.

What Hamlet has not discovered from the grave digger, dawns upon him as the funeral cortège appears upon the scene, bringing the mortal remains of Ophelia for burial. Her interment is preceded by a heated argument between the officiating priest, who has not accorded her full Christian burial rites because of the suspicion of suicide, and Laertes, who is greatly enraged at such clerical intolerance. His anger, however, is not only directed at the priest. After the Queen, with words of sympathy and sorrow, has strewn flowers upon the coffin, Laertes, breaking out in wild denunciation of Hamlet, whom he holds to be the real murderer of Ophelia, leaps into the grave and demands that he shall be buried with his sister. This is too much for Hamlet, who has until now remained in the background with Horatio. He springs forward with challenging words and a moment later is struggling desperately with Laertes in the grave. The horrified spectators attempt to separate them, while the Queen and Horatio try to calm Hamlet.

The spectators do not doubt that they are witnessing an outbreak of madness, and there is no need for the Queen, who is deeply troubled, to beg them to be patient until it is over. Hamlet's excitement quickly dies down but he still remains with a sense of deep injury for, as he says, he has always had a certain affection for Ophelia's brother. This feeling, however, does not prevent him from leaving the scene with a very contemptuous reference to Laertes.

The King, who as usual has cautiously remained all the time in the background, enjoins Laertes to be patient, and remember their plan.

ACT V SCENE 1

NOTES:

192   See Note No. 67.

193   Mrs. Siddons appears to hold the honour of being the first female Hamlet, although no contemporary surprise seems to have been aroused when she played the part in Manchester as early as 1777. Her appearance there on March 19th was billed as her second time in the part. She never appeared in the character in London, though she was still playing it as late as 1802, when an appearance is recorded in Dublin on July 27th. She was always self-conscious of displaying her figure, and wore a "shawl-like garment" for the part. Mrs. Siddons only once played Ophelia, to the Hamlet of John Philip Kemble at Drury Lane in 1786. Her first London appearance as Gertrude was to Richard Wroughton's Hamlet in 1796, but she did not often repeat the part.

194   Master Betty, "The Young Roscius", first appeared in London at Covent Garden in 1804. He was twelve years old. The following year he played Hamlet at Drury Lane. Other boy actors, including Master W. R. Grossmith (c. 1825), and Master Joseph Burke (c. 1829), played the part. The latter also played Hamlet in New York (1831).

195   Etching by George Cruikshank to illustrate an incident in *Memoirs of Grimaldi* by "Boz" (Charles Dickens) 1838. (See Note No. 148.)

196   See Note No. 1.

197   See Note No. 2.

198   See Note No. 3.

199   The model theatre and scenery published from about 1840 to 1860 by M. Trentsensky of Vienna is almost the most elaborate and artistic work of its kind. The scenes are finely engraved and hand-coloured. They are of the most popular plays and operas of the time, and are faithful reproductions of the scenery in contemporary use at the Vienna Opera House. They are described as being from the designs of T. Jachimovicz and others. Jachimovicz was a famous Vienna scenic artist, he worked at the Carltheater and the Josefstadter between 1827 and 1851 and during that period was responsible for many of the most elaborate productions of the era.

200   Josef Kainz, a Hungarian-born German actor trained with the Saxe-Meiningen Company. This company, founded by the Duke of Saxe-Meiningen (1826–1914), established a theatre in which the effect was that of a team rather than that of an individual actor. Under him the producer rose to be the principal influence rather than the players; he combined accurate costumes, scenery (by Israel and Libermann) together with the production, into a complete unity. His company toured nine countries between 1874 and 1890; they were in London at Drury Lane in 1881 for a season, and its influence was seen in many subsequent productions throughout the world. Benson founded his company in 1883 on the Saxe-Meiningen model. It is interesting to note that Friedrich von Bodenstedt, who was the big influence behind the Duke, saw the Charles Kean revivals in London and reported to the Duke, before he embarked on his epoch-making productions. Ludwig Barney played Hamlet with this company, but it was not included in the London Season.
    See also Note No. 171.

201   See Note No. 3.

202   There have been some notable Hamlets in the Swedish theatre, particularly Gösta Eckman and Lars Hanson in recent years.

203   See Note No. 75.

204   See Note No. 15.

205   See Note No. 43.

206 and 207   See Note No. 50.

208   See Note No. 58.

209   See Note No. 108.

210   See Note No. 113.

211   See Note No. 53.

212 See Note No. 121
213 See Note No. 79.
214 See Note No. 18.
215 See Note No. 162. Akimov transferred the Grave Diggers scene to Hamlet's Study.
216 See Note No. 127.
217 and 218 See Note No. 19.
219 See Note No. 8.
220 This was the first production of *Hamlet* on television. The Ophelia was Muriel Pavlov. See also No. 249. John Byron played Hamlet at Stratford (see Note No. 123 and No. 134).
221 See Note No. 25.
222 See Note No. 168.
223 See Note No. 10.
224 See Note No. 136.

Mary Bolton as Ophelia, after a drawing by Samuel de Wilde, published 1813. She first appeared in the part at Covent Garden Theatre, London, in 1807, to the Hamlet of John Philip Kemble, and remained his Ophelia till her retirement in 1813. She also played the part with Charles Kemble in 1812.

It is interesting to note that although Kemble had, in 1783, introduced a stage Elizabethan costume for Hamlet, his Ophelia was still continuing to dress in contemporary fashion. (See Note No. 175.)

ACT V SCENE 1

192 London, Haymarket Theatre, 1777. Hamlet: John Henderson.

193 Dublin, Theatre Royal, 1802. Sarah Siddons' costume as Hamlet. From a water-colour drawing in Mary Hamilton's collection of "Dresses and Attitudes of Mrs. Siddons," in the British Museum.

194 London, Theatre Royal, Drury Lane, 1805. Hamlet: Master William Betty, "The Young Roscius".

195 *Hamlet* in a northern provincial theatre, c. 1800. Hamlet: John Philip Kemble. First Grave Digger: "Jew" Davis.

196 Juvenile Drama Scene, published by West, London, 1815. Backcloth and wing.

197 London, Princess's Theatre, 1850. Set drawing by H. Cuthbert from a design by Thomas Grieve, for Charles Kean's production.

ACT V SCENE 1

198 London, Lyceum Theatre, 1864. (Hamlet: Charles Fechter.) Set design by William Telbin, Snr.

198. Austria, model theatre with scenery made between 1840 and 1850 by Trentsensky. Set probably designed by Jachimovicz.

126　　　　　　　　　　　　　　　　　　　　　　　　　　　　　HAMLET THROUGH THE AGES

200 Germany, Berlin, Neues Schauspielhaus, 1909. Hamlet: Joseph Kainz. Settings by Svend Gade, costumes by Professor Lefler.

201 London, Princess's Theatre, 1861. Hamlet: Charles Fechter. First Grave Digger: Henry Widdicombe. Produced by Charles Fechter, settings by James Gates, Mr. Neville and W. Broadfoot.

202 Sweden, Stockholm, National Theatre, 1920. Hamlet: Gösta Eckman.

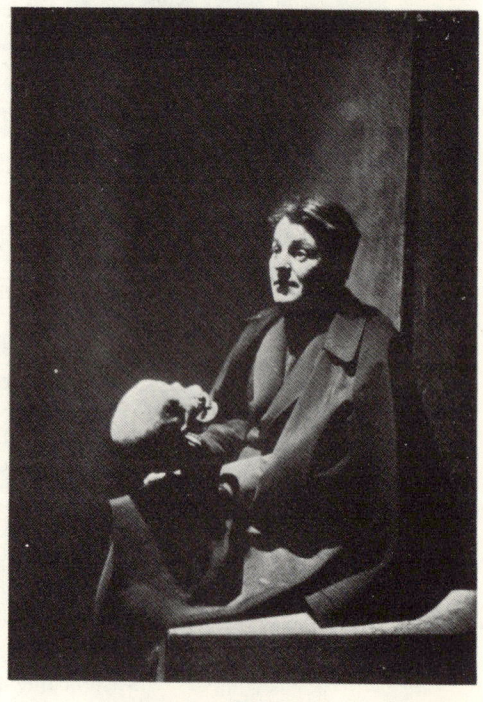

203 Austria, Vienna, Deutsches Volkstheater, 1926. Hamlet: Alexander Moissi. Produced by H. K. Ayliff, settings by Paul Shelving.

ACT V SCENE 1

204 Germany, Mannheim, Court Theatre, 1907. Set design by Carl Hagemann.

205 London, Lyceum Theatre, 1909. Hamlet: Matheson Lang. Horatio: Halliwell Hobbs.
First Grave Digger: S. Major Jones. Produced by Ernest Carpenter, settings by E. C. Nicholls.

206 Germany, Berlin, Deutsches Theater, 1909. Hamlet: Alexander Moissi. Horatio: Eduard von Winterstein. Produced by Max Reinhardt, settings by Ernst Stern.

207 Germany, Berlin, Deutsches Theater, 1909. (Hamlet: Alexander Moissi.) First Grave Digger: Hans Pagay. Second Grave Digger: Ernst Lubitsch. Produced by Max Reinhardt, settings by Ernst Stern.

208 Poland, Warsaw, Polski Theatre, 1947. (Hamlet: Marian Wyrsykoski.) The Two Grave Diggers. Produced by Arnold Szyffman, settings by Karol Frycz.

ACT V SCENE 1

209 London, Royal Opera House, Covent Garden, 1919. Hamlet: Martin Harvey. Produced by Martin Harvey, production designed by Martin Harvey.

210 London, Kingsway Theatre (Barry Jackson's Birmingham Repertory Company), 1925. Hamlet: Colin Keith-Johnson. Priest: Frank Denis. Horatio: Alan Howland. Claudius: Frank Vosper. Gertrude: Dorothy Massingham. Laertes: Robert Holmes. Produced by H. K. Ayliff, settings and costumes by Paul Shelving.

211 Czechoslovakia Prague, National Theatre, 1926. Set design by Vlastial Hofman.

212 Czechoslovakia, Prague, Municipal Theatre, 1927. Hamlet: Zdenek Stepanek. Produced by Yaroslav Kvapil, settings by Josef Wenig.

ACT V SCENE 1

213 Germany, Berlin State Theatre, 1927. Hamlet: Fritz Kortner. Horatio: Günther Hadank. Produced by Leopold Jessner, settings by Caspar Neher.

214 London, New Theatre, 1934. Hamlet: John Gielgud. First Grave Digger: Ben Field. Horatio: Jack Hawkins. Produced by John Gielgud, settings and costumes by Motley.

215 U.S.S.R., Moscow, Vahtangov Theatre, 1931. Hamlet: Gorunov. Production and settings by Nicolai Akimov.

216 London, Old Vic, 1937. Hamlet: Laurence Olivier. Laertes: Michael Redgrave. Claudius: Francis L. Sullivan. Gertrude: Dorothy Dix. Priest: Neville Mapp. Produced by Tyrone Guthrie, settings by Martin Battersby, costumes by Osborne Robinson.

ACT V SCENE 1

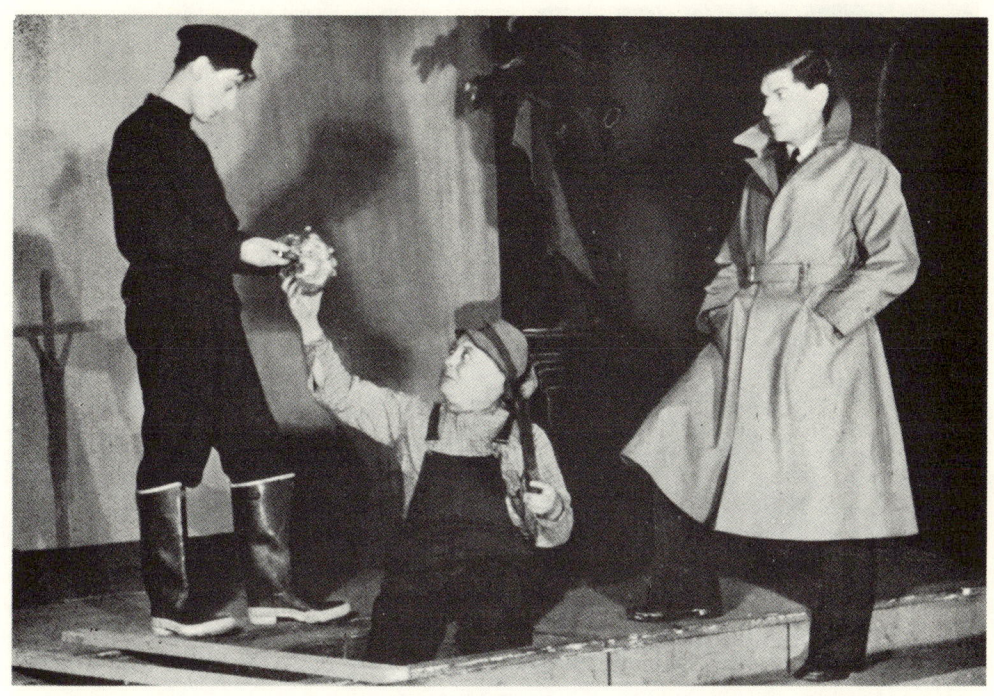

217 London, Old Vic, 1938. Hamlet: Alec Guinness. First Grave Digger: Frank Tickle. Horatio: André Morell. Produced by Tyrone Guthrie, settings and costumes by Roger Furse.

218 London, Old Vic, 1938. (Hamlet: Alec Guinness.) Laertes: Anthony Quayle. Claudius: Andrew Cruickshank. Gertrude: Veronica Turleigh. Priest: Philip Bowen. Produced by Tyrone Guthrie, settings and costumes by Roger Furse.

219 London, Arts Theatre, 1945. (Hamlet: Alec Clunes.) Produced by Judith Furse, settings by Michael Warre.

220 London, Television (B.B.C.), 1947. Hamlet: John Byron. Horatio: Patrick Troughton. Grave Digger: Jay Laurier. Produced by George More O'Farrell, settings by Peter Bax.

ACT V SCENE 1

221 London, New Theatre (Old Vic Company), 1944. Hamlet: Robert Helpmann. Horatio: Dennis Price. First Grave Digger: Gus McNaughton. Produced by Tyrone Guthrie and Michael Benthall, settings and costumes by Leslie Hurry.

222 London, Haymarket Theatre, 1944. Hamlet: John Gielgud. Horatio: Francis Lister. Claudius: Leslie Banks. Gertrude: Marian Spencer. Grave Digger: George Woodbridge. Produced by George Rylands. Settings by Ruth Keating, costumes by Jeanetta Cochrane.

223 England, Two Cities Film for the J. Arthur Rank Organization, 1948. Hamlet: Laurence Olivier. Horatio: Norman Wooland. First Grave Digger: Stanley Holloway. Directed by Laurence Olivier, settings and costumes by Roger Furse.

224 England, Stratford-upon-Avon, Memorial Theatre, 1948. Hamlet: Paul Scofield (alternating with Robert Helpmann). First Grave Digger: Esmond Knight. Horatio: John Justin. Produced by Michael Benthall, settings and costumes by James Bailey.

Act V Scene 2

A HALL IN THE CASTLE

(In acting editions, particularly in the nineteenth and twentieth centuries when scenery was cumbersome and productions heavy, this scene was divided into two parts to allow the Graveyard to be cleared and the Hall set ; to do this the Osric scene was played as in a room in the Castle, a frontcloth being used ; the second part in the Hall of the Castle commencing with the entrance of Claudius and his Court)

It is not until Hamlet and Horatio meet again in this scene that Hamlet explains the reason for his unexpected return, and how he changed the letter to England demanding his death to one which asked for the execution of Rosencrantz and Guildenstern instead. As for taking revenge upon his uncle he declares that he has no longer any scruples of conscience on that score. Horatio warns him that it is now all the more urgent to carry out his intention, because the news of the execution of the two, Rosencrantz and Guildenstern, must soon arrive. Hamlet reassures him; his mind is made up, but he adds a few words of regret, in passing, at his own impassioned conduct towards Laertes at Ophelia's grave. It grieves him all the more, because he sees in Laertes' fate a parallel to his own, and feels a real sympathy for him.

Particulars of the fencing match are now given to Hamlet by a messenger sent by the King, the effeminate young courtier Osric, who is to act as referee.

In the serene mood that has now come over Hamlet it is not hard for him, when the Court enters to attend the fencing match, to make some friendly gesture to Laertes—an action especially desired of him in a message sent by his mother. Laertes makes a show of accepting the reconciliation, but with a skilfully formulated reservation which in reality means that he binds himself to nothing; the King outdoes himself in false and exaggerated courtesy, affecting to take the warmest personal interest in Hamlet's triumph by offering valuable rewards and arranging for the shooting off of ordnance. But chance plays the murderer a double trick. Hamlet does not, as expected, after his first successful bout, take from the King's own hand the goblet in which he has poured a deadly poison in place of the valuable pearl of which he spoke; but, impatient as usual, begins the second bout. The unsuspicious Queen, however, anxious for her heated, overtired and sweating son and wishing to show her solicitude for him offers to wipe the moisture from his brow with her own handkerchief, and then tries to hearten him by drinking his health in the poisoned goblet. The warning cry of her horrified husband comes too late. In the meantime Hamlet and Laertes have continued to attack one another more impetuously, their foils in their right hands and their daggers in their left. Laertes, a better fencer than Hamlet, has been playing with him for some time, without allowing the Prince to notice it; he now assaults in earnest and succeeds in wounding him, as foreseen, with the poisoned foil. Hamlet, angered at this, does all he

ACT V SCENE 2   137

can to improve his play. It appears that he skilfully disarms Laertes, and that Laertes seizes Hamlet's weapon, whereupon the Prince, under cover of his dagger, bends, picks up his opponent's foil and continues to use it in the bout. With the next lunge Laertes is wounded with his own poisoned foil. At the same moment the Queen sinks to the ground. Even now the King attempts to save the situation by a lie, but the Queen reveals the truth and with her last breath, cries out to her son with motherly tenderness. Hamlet has shaken off much of his apathy in the excitement of the bout and the sudden horrible realization that his own death was intended restores to him all his strength and forethought. He tries to make himself master of the situation by giving orders to the guards but it is too late. Laertes, knowing that his own moments are numbered, tells him the whole horrible truth. He points to the King as the instigator of all the treachery. Hamlet at last exerts his remaining strength and turns his weapon on the King. And when the King, unyielding to the last, calls for help despite his deadly wound Hamlet falls on him with rage, flinging his villainy in his face, and forces him, with mocking words, to drink the remains of his own poisoned cup. The dying Laertes sees in the death of this man, who has used him as his tool, only an act of justice, as he pays his last tribute to Hamlet's noble nature; their guilt is equal. Hamlet, too, now feels the approach of death. His dying words are addressed to Horatio, whom he seeks to restrain from suicide by charging him to inform the world of what has taken place. When he hears of the coming of Fortinbras, whom chance now brings on to the scene of the tragedy, he repeats his request that Fortinbras, whose great heritage he in no way grudges, shall be told everything. Death cuts short his words but he is able at the point of death to sum up everything in a few splendidly impersonal and ironic words: " The rest is silence ".

With the death of Hamlet the tragedy ends. Norwegian Fortinbras at once decides to seize the land, now left without a ruler. At this moment the ambassadors from England return with the tidings of the death of Rosencrantz and Guildenstern. Horatio's wish that the whole sad story should be made public is readily granted by the new King, who accords Hamlet, for his burial, the highest military honours.

NOTES:

225 and 226   Frontcloths used for the Osric scene.
  See also Notes Nos. 1 and 2.

227   See Note No. 1.

228   See Note No. 2.

229   See Note No. 103.

230   See Note No. 30.

231   See Note No. 107.

232   Forbes Robertson played the Death scene seated on the throne; he was assisted there by Horatio, who, after Hamlet's death, placed Claudius's crown on the dead Prince's lap. The final scene with Fortinbras was restored to the text. In the version which had been used for many years the play had always ended at Hamlet's last words, " The rest is silence ". (See Note No. 107.)

233 See Note No. 108.
234 See Note No. 6.
235 See Note No. 50.
236 See Note No. 113.
237 See Note No. 77.
238 See Note No. 18.
239 See Note No. 53.
240 See Note No. 121.

241 See Note No. 163. After a lapse of some 20 years Hamlet was again produced in Moscow in Jan. 1955 at the Mayakousky Theatre with Evgeny Samoilov as the Prince. It was directed by Nikolai Okhlopkov with settings and costumes by V. Ryndin. A report says "Shakespeare's finest tragedy so long falsified by bourgeois art is being given a new production which shows Hamlet in the centre of the struggle for world culture. An essential link in this great struggle, he once again confirms the indispensable truth that only a forward, progressive ideology can preserve and multiply the spiritual values of popular genius."

242 This production was used again at Stratford in 1940 with a new cast (see No. 128). Donald Wolfit has since played Hamlet with his own company. He first played the part in London at the Kingsway Theatre in 1940 and included a revival of the play in most of his subsequent seasons. He also played the part in Canada and New York, 1947.

243 See Note No. 127.

244 See Note No. 19.

245 J. Grant Anderson's Indian National Theatre Company toured India for some years and was the training ground for many native artists. Another Empire production was in South Africa in 1947, when André Huguenet appeared as Hamlet in an Afrikaans translation of the play.

246 See Note No. 10.

247 This production, with a new setting, visited Elsinore (see No. 57). Michael Redgrave played Laertes at the Old Vic and at Elsinore with Laurence Olivier in 1937 (see No. 55).

248 This was the Festival of Britain year *Hamlet*. It was an interpretation which aroused more controversy, for and against, than any production in recent years. Alec Guinness, who had previously played the part in modern dress at the Old Vic (see Note No. 19), is shown in the photograph with a beard. He changed his make-up during the short run of the production.

249 See No. 220.

250 In the ballet version, the story of *Hamlet* is seen through the mind of the dying Hamlet. The ballet opens and closes on the same situation, seen in the photograph. The part of Hamlet in the ballet was created by its choreographer, Robert Helpmann. It has been included in the repertoire of the Sadler's Wells Ballet Company at Covent Garden. The music used is Tchaikovsky's *Fantasia Overture*.

Hamlet as a ballet is not a new medium for staging the story. A version was danced at the San Carlo, Naples, in 1824. Bronislava Nijinska also produced a version of her own in Paris in 1934.

Another *Hamlet* ballet was produced in Munich (1950) with choreography by Victor Gsovsky, décor by Rosemarie Jakameit and music by Boris Blacher. The Hamlet was danced by Franz Bauer, and Ophelia by Irene Skorik. This ballet has been revived with a new décor and choreography in Buenos Aires, Colon Theatre (September 1951).

251 See page 94.

252
253 } The translation was by Luigi Squarzina.

254 See Note No. 19. The Ophelia was Claire Bloom.

255 See Note No. 55.

ACT V SCENE 2

225 Juvenile Drama Scene, published by West, London, 1815. Backcloth and wing.

226 London, Princess's Theatre, 1850. Set drawing by Jones from a design by Thomas Grieve for Charles Kean's production.

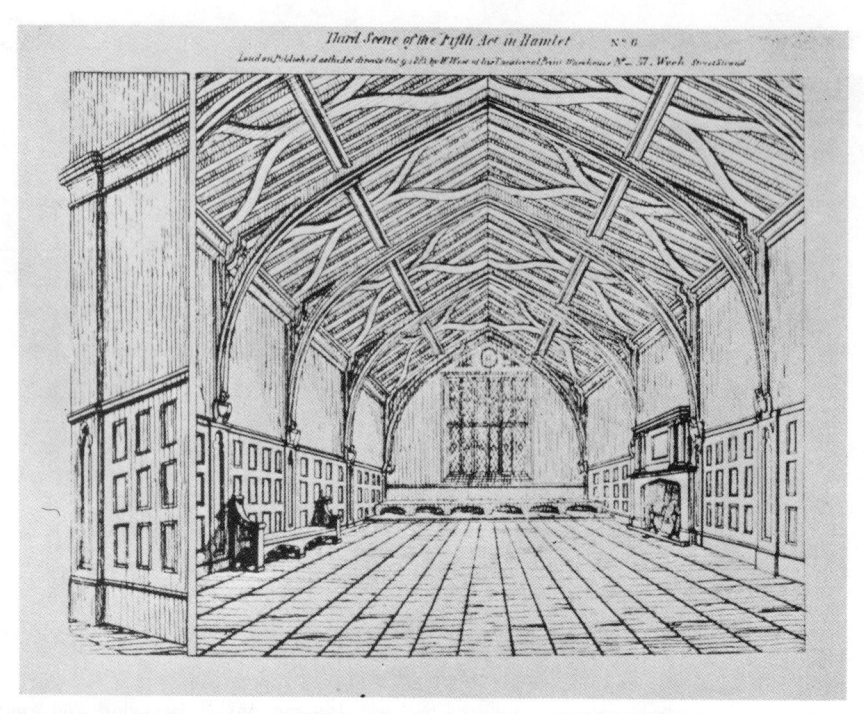

227 Juvenile Drama Set, published by West, London, 1815. Backcloth and wing.

228 London, Princess's Theatre, 1850. Set drawing by Jones from a design by Thomas Grieve for Charles Kean's production.

ACT V SCENE 2

229 Juvenile Drama Set, published by Hodgson, London, between 1822 and 1830.

230 London, Covent Garden Theatre, 1838. Hamlet: William Charles Macready. Laertes: James Anderson. Claudius: Charles Diddear. Gertrude: Mary Warner (Miss Huddart). Horatio: William Searle. Produced by William Charles Macready.

231 London, Theatre Royal, Drury Lane, 1913. Hamlet: Forbes Robertson. Gertrude: Adeline Bourne. Laertes: Alex Scott-Gatty. Claudius: Walter Ringham. Horatio: S. A. Cookson. Produced by Forbes Robertson, settings by Hawes Craven, costumes by Karl.

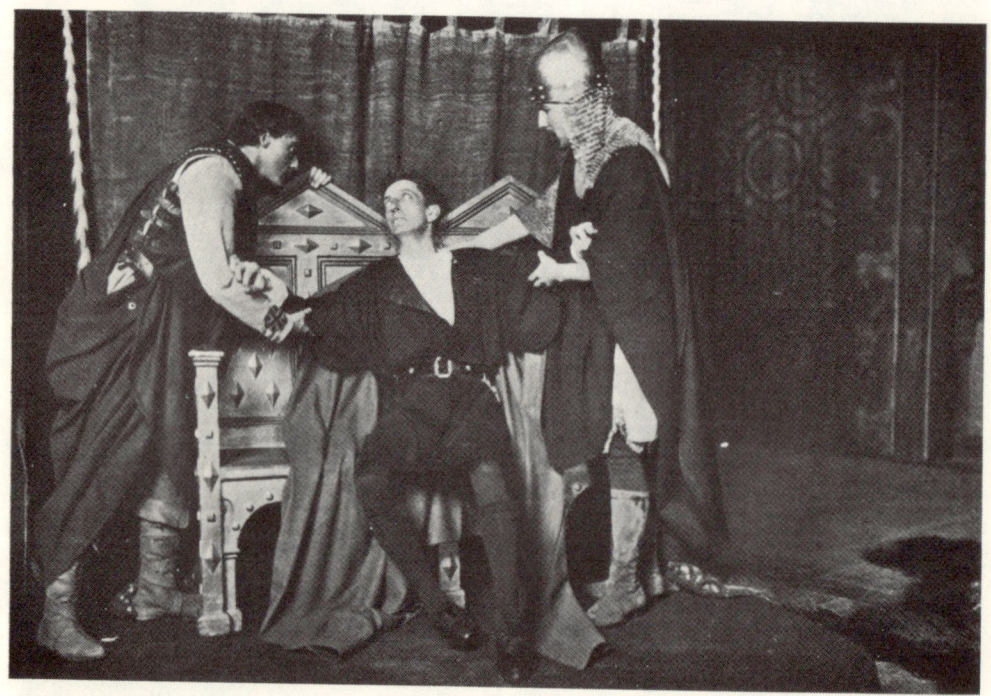

232 London, Theatre Royal, Drury Lane, 1913. Hamlet: Forbes Robertson. Horatio: S. A. Cookson. Produced by Forbes Robertson, settings by Hawes Craven, costumes by Karl.

ACT V SCENE 2

233 London, Lyric Theatre, 1905. Hamlet: Martin Harvey. Gertrude: Maud Milton. Horatio: Percy Anstey. Claudius: Charles Glenny. Laertes: Charles Lander. Produced by Martin Harvey, settings by George J. Dodson.

234 Germany, Dresden, Court Theatre, 1909. Produced by Ernst Lewinger, settings by Fritz Schumacher.

235 Germany, Berlin, Deutsches Theater, 1909. Hamlet: Alexander Moissi. Horatio: Eduard von Winterstein. Claudius: Paul Wagener. Gertrude: Rosa Bertens. Produced by Max Reinhardt, settings by Ernst Stern.

236 London, Kingsway Theatre (Barry Jackson's Birmingham Repertory Company), 1925. Hamlet: Colin Keith-Johnston. Laertes: Robert Holmes. Horatio: Alan Howland. Gertrude: Dorothy Massingham. Claudius: Frank Vosper. Produced by H. K. Ayliff, settings and costumes by Paul Shelving.

ACT V SCENE 2

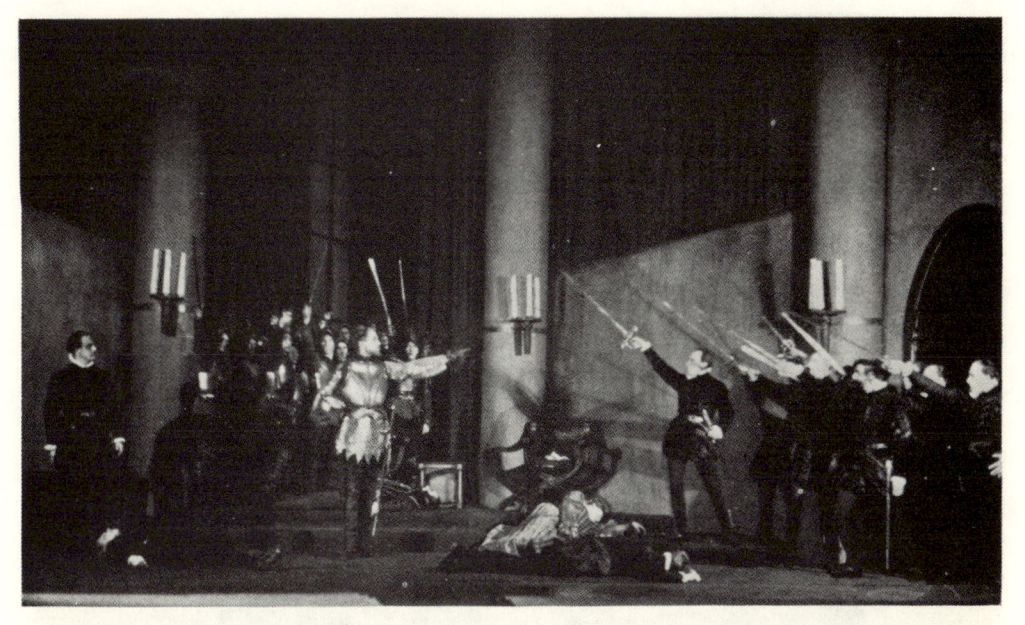

237 Germany, Dresden, State Theatre, 1927. Hamlet: Steinböck. Horatio: Paulsen. Fortinbras: Heinz Woester. Claudius: Willy Kleinoschegg. Gertrude: Volckmar. Produced by Gerhart Hauptmann, settings by Adolf Mahnke.

238 London, New Theatre, 1934. Hamlet: John Gielgud. Laertes: Glen Byam Shaw. Osric: Alec Guinness. Fortinbras: Geoffrey Toone. Horatio: Jack Hawkins. Gertrude: Laura Cowie. Produced by John Gielgud, settings and costumes by Motley.

239 Czechoslovakia, Prague, National Theatre, 1926. Set design by Vlastial Hofman.

240 Czechoslovakia, Prague, Municipal Theatre, 1927. Hamlet: Zdenek Stepanek. Produced by Yaroslav Kvapil. Settings by Josef Wenig.

ACT V SCENE 2

241 U.S.S.R., Moscow, Vahtangov Theatre, 1931. Hamlet: Gorunov. Production and settings by Nicolai Akimov.

242 England, Stratford-upon-Avon, Memorial Theatre, 1937. Hamlet: Donald Wolfit. Gertrude: Clare Harris. Claudius: Norman Wooland. Laertes: Godfrey Kenton. Produced by Iden Payne, settings by Randle Ayrton, costumes by Barbara Curtis.

243 London, Old Vic, 1937. Hamlet: Laurence Olivier. Claudius: Francis L. Sullivan. Gertrude: Dorothy Dix. Produced by Tyrone Guthrie, settings by Martin Battersby, costumes by Osborne Robinson.

244 London, Old Vic, 1938. Hamlet: Alec Guinness. Osric: John Kidd. Gertrude: Veronica Turleigh. Claudius: Andrew Cruickshank. Laertes: Anthony Quayle. Produced by Tyrone Guthrie, settings and costumes by Roger Furse.

ACT V SCENE 2

245 India, Bombay, Opera House (The Indian National Theatre Company), 1931. Hamlet: J. Grant Anderson, with a cast of Indian artists. Produced by J. Grant Anderson, settings and costumes by Gladstone Solomons.

246 England, Two Cities Film for the J. Arthur Rank Organization, 1948. Hamlet: Laurence Olivier. Horatio: Norman Wooland. Gertrude: Eileen Herlie. Claudius: Basil Sydney. Laertes: Terence Morgan. Directed by Laurence Olivier, settings and costumes by Roger Furse.

247 London, New Theatre (Old Vic Company), 1950. Hamlet: Michael Redgrave. Laertes: Peter Copley. Claudius: Mark Dignam. Gertrude: Wanda Rotha. Osric: Paul Rogers. Produced by Hugh Hunt, settings and costumes by Laurence Irving.

248 London, New Theatre, 1951. Hamlet: Alec Guinness. Laertes: Michael Gough. Claudius: Walter Fitzgerald. Gertrude: Lydia Sherwood. Produced by Alec Guinness and Frank Hauser, settings and costumes by Mariano Andreu.

ACT V SCENE 2

249 London, Television (B.B.C.), 1947. Hamlet: John Byron. Laertes: Patrick Macnee. Claudius: Sebastian Shaw. Gertrude: Margaret Rawlings. Produced by George More O'Farrell, settings by Peter Bax.

250 London, New Theatre (Sadler's Wells Ballet Company), 1942. Hamlet: Robert Helpmann. Claudius: David Paltenghi. Gertrude: Celia Franca. Laertes: John Hart. Ballet in one scene by Robert Helpmann to the music of Tchaikovsky's *Hamlet Fantasia Overture*. Setting and costumes by Leslie Hurry.

251 Act III, Scene 2, Germany, Bochum, Parktheater, 1952. Hamlet: Hans Messemer. Horatio: Walter Kaltheuner. Ophelia: Rosel Schaefer. Polonius: Robert Lossen. Player Queen: Eva-Katharina Schultz. Player King: Max Nemetz. Rosencranz: Manfred Heidmann. Guildenstern: Alexander May. King Claudius: Hans-Ernst Jäger. Gertrude: Ursula von Reibnitz. Produced by Hans Schalla. Settings by Max Fritzsche. Costumes by Therese van Treeck.

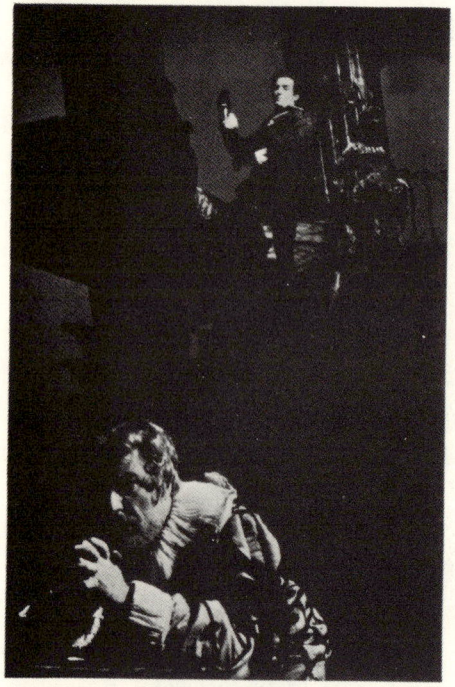

252 Act III, Scene 3, Italy, Rome, Teatro Valle, 1952. Hamlet: Vittorio Gassman. Claudius: Mario Feliciani. Produced by Vittorio Gassman. Costumes and settings by Mario Chiari. (See page 138.)

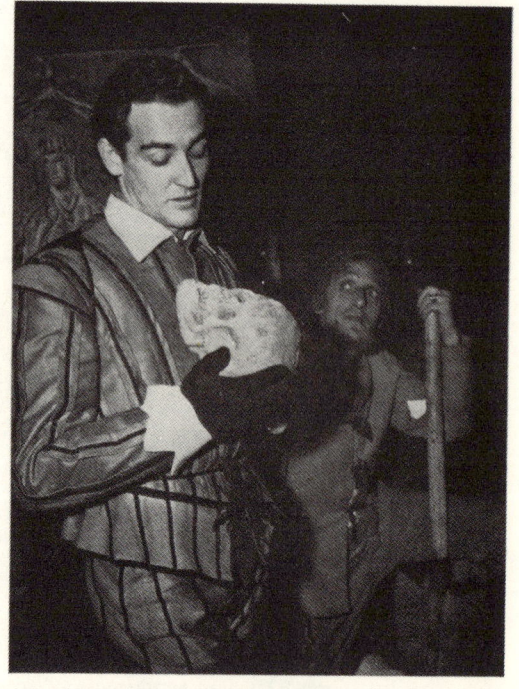

253 Act V, Scene 1. Italy, Rome, Teatro Valle, 1952. Hamlet: Vittorio Gassman. First Gravedigger: Ferruccio Stagni. Produced by Vittorio Gassman. Costumes and settings by Mario Chiari.

ACT V SCENE 2

254 Act V, Scene 2. London, Old Vic, 1953. Hamlet: Richard Burton. Claudius: Laurence Hardy. Osric: Timothy Bateson. Fortinbras: John Neville. Horatio: William Squire. Gertrude: Fay Compton. Laertes: Robert Hardy. Produced by Michael Benthall. Settings by Kenneth Rowell, with a permanent façade and proscenium by James Bailey. (See page 11.)

255 Act I, Scene 2. Denmark, Elsinore, Kronborg Castle (Old Vic Company), 1954. Hamlet: Richard Burton. Gertrude: Fay Compton. Claudius: Laurence Hardy. Polonius: Michael Hordern. Produced by Michael Benthall. Setting and costumes by Kenneth Rowell. (See page 11.)

Index

(All Numbers refer to Pages)

HAMLETS

Ainley, Henry, 3, 68, 81
Aldridge, Ira, 69
Anderson, J. Grant, 149
Bandmann, Daniel, 2
Bandmann-Palmer, Mrs., 24
Bannister, John, 28
Barney, Ludwig, 2, 121
Barrault, Jean-Louis, 39, 49
Barrett, Laurence, 2
Barrett, Wilson, 61, 62
Barry, Spranger, 93, 95
Barrymore, John, 2, 3, 10, 15, 63, 77, 118
Bartley, Mrs., 24
Bauer, Franz, 138
Bennett, John, 91
Benson, Frank, 25, 34, 69
Bernhardt, Sarah, 3, 24, 49, 52, 69
Berringer, Esmé, 24
Betterton, Thomas, 93
Betty, Master William, 121, 123
Booth, Edwin, 2, 104, 111
Booth, J. B., 2
Breen, Robert, 26
Brockman, Johann, 67, 70, 95
Burbage, Richard, 93
Burke, Joseph, 121
Burton, Richard, 11, 153
Büttner, Wolfgang, 85
Byron, John, 69, 86, 122, 134, 151
Carrington, Murray, 69
Caspar, Horst, 49
Chekov, Michael, 77
Clunes, Alec, 2, 7, 16, 21, 65, 110, 134
Cooke, George Frederick, 2
Craig, Gordon, 25
Creswick, William, 24, 33
Cushman, Charlotte, 24
Deutsch, Ernst, 53
Devrients, Emile, 49
Dillon, Charles, *frontispiece*
Eddison, Robert, 65, 87
Eckman, Gösta, 121, 126
Evans, Maurice, 2, 3, 11, 69, 86
Fauré, 32
Fechter, Charles, 1, 5, 13, 31, 97, 125, 126
Fujisawa, Ajiro, 35, 74, 113
Garrick, David, 23, 28, 61, 93
Gassman, Vittorio, 152
Gielgud, John, 2, 3, 10, 11, 15, 26, 40, 41, 69, 82, 90, 104, 105, 117, 118, 131, 135, 145
Glenville, Peter, 17, 20, 55
Glover, Julia, 24
Goring, Marius, 11
Gorunov, 102, 132, 147
Gould, Nutcombe, 25
Greet, Ben, 3

Grétillat, Jacques, 3, 100
Grossmith, Master W. R., 121
Gründgens, Gustaf, 26, 61, 65
Guinness, Alec, 11, 16, 43, 56, 57, 58, 133, 138, 148, 151
Hallam, Thomas, 2
Hampden, Walter, 2, 7, 64, 100
Hanson, Lars, 121
Harris, Robert, 11, 27, 43, 81
Harvey, Martin, 68, 69, 73, 75, 115, 129, 143
Harvey, Rupert, 11
Hayes, George, 69
Heath, Gordon, 85
Helpmann, Robert, 18, 21, 57, 58, 69, 87, 103, 135, 151
Henderson, John, 61, 67, 70, 93, 96, 123
Hidoyatov, 84, 101
Holloway, Baliol, 11
Howard, Clara, 24
Howard, Leslie, 2, 23, 69, 108
Huguenet, André, 138
Inchbald, Mrs. Eliza, 24
Irving, H. B., 13, 20, 69
Irving, Henry, 2, 25, 33, 52, 112, 113
Johnson, Henry Erskine, 48, 50, 61, 62
Jones, George (" Count Johannes "), 2
Judith, Madame, 49
Kainz, Joseph, 109, 121, 126
Katchaloff, Vassily, 36, 52, 74
Kean, Charles, 2, 24, 27, 31, 48, 51, 104
Kean, Edmund, 2, 3, 11, 23, 24, 29, 50
Kearns, Mr., 24
Keith-Johnson, Colin, 76, 102, 129, 144
Kemble, Charles, 2, 61, 122
Kemble, John Philip, 61, 93, 96, 121, 122, 123
Kemble, Stephen, 61, 62
Kohout, Edward, 26, 39
Kortner, Fritz, 55, 78, 131
Krolikowski, 113
Lacy, W. W., 24
Lang, Matheson, 25, 34, 69, 107, 116, 127
Langton, Basil, 69, 83
Laurie, John, 11, 69
Le Gallienne, Eva, 24
Lindström, Erik, 26
Mac Liammóir, Michael, 26
McMaster, Anew, 69
Macready, William Charles, 2, 23 29, 71, 96, 141
Markham, David, 49
Marriott, Alice, 24, 33
Massey, Raymond, 2, 44
Matthews, Tom, 24
Messemer, Hans, 94, 152
Milton, Ernest, 11, 18

Minotis, 49
Moissi, Alexander, 3, 25, 38, 49, 53, 75, 99, 126 128, 144
Molchanov, P., 56
Mounet-Sully, Jean, 49, 52
Murray, Stephen, 68
Nedbal, Milos, 68
Neuff, Alwin, 3
Nilsen, Asta, 3, 61
Nilsen, Hans Jacob, 26
O'Brien, Terence, 11
Olivier, Laurence, 3, 8, 11, 26, 40, 59, 83, 91, 103, 118, 132, 135, 138 148, 149
Pallin, Ingemar, 26
Payne, John Howard, 2
Percy, Esmé, 11, 112
Phelps, Samuel, 93, 96
Phillips, Arthur, 69
Poel, William, 112
Powell, Mrs., 24
Redgrave, Michael, 11, 26, 41, 151
Robertson, Forbes, 2–3, 8, 14, 37, 68, 69, 73, 98, 114, 116, 137, 142
Ross, David, 48, 50
Ross, Eric, 11
Rossi, Ernesto, 2, 49
Ruggeri, Ruggero, 49
Salvini, Tomaso, 2, 49
Samoilov, Evgeny, 138
Santley, Charles, 24
Scofield, Paul, 69, 87, 135
Siddons, Sarah, 24, 61, 121, 123
Slavzo, Jan, 59
Smith, William (" Gentleman "), 111, 113
Speaight, Robert, 11, 27
Stack, William, 11, 69
Steinböck, Felix, 55, 117, 145
Stepanek, Zdenek, 80, 103, 110, 130, 146
Sullivan, Barry, 48, 51, 69
Swinley, Ion, 11, 25
Sydney, Basil, 88
Talma, 61, 93
Tearle, Godfrey, 69
Thorndike, Russell, 11
Togoz, Zyomimir, 26
Tree, H. Beerbohm, 67, 69, 72, 112
Warburton, Charles, 11
Wilkes, Robert, 67, 70
Wolfit, Donald, 69, 138, 147
Wroughton, Richard, 121
Wrzykowski, Marian, 42, 54, 91, 101, 128
Wyse, John, 112
Yarrow, Duncan, 11
Young, Charles Mayne, 27, 61, 62
Young, James, 3

ACTORS (APPEARING IN OTHER CHARACTERS)

Adamson, Joseph, 20, 55
Adeca, Dorothy, 85
Aherne, Elena, 76
Aldridge, Michael, 41
Allestree, Mary, 116
Andean, Richard, 8
Anderson, James, 141
Anderson, Judith, 82
Andrews, Harry, 82
Anstey, Percy, 73, 143
Argles, John, 55
Arthur, L., 73
Asche, Oscar, 13
Atkins, Robert, 8, 37
Aylmer, Felix, 59
Banks, Leslie, 105, 135
Barnes, J. H., 14, 73

Barry, Mrs., 93
Barry, Mrs. Spranger (Ann), 93, 95
Bateman, Isabel, 25
Bateson, Timothy, 153
Beazley, Sam, 82
Benson, George, 41
Bertens, Rosa, 75, 99, 144
Betterton, Mrs. (Mary Saunderson), 93
Bildt, Paul, 49, 55
Blair, Lionel, 86
Bland, Zoe, 115
Bloom, Claire, 87, 138
Boleslavsky, R. V., 74
Bolton, Mary, 122
Bourne, Adeline, 14, 73, 142
Bowen, Philip, 133
Bracki, Wladyslaw, 42
Brayton, Lily, 20

Brigg-Hall, Austin, 85
Britton, Hutin, 116
Bromley-Davenport, A., 76, 102
Browne, Pamela, 21
Brückner, Johannes, 70
Bryan, Peggy, 83
Brydone, Alfred, 34
Buckle, Richard, 55
Burden, Anna, 86
Burge, Stuart, 83
Byron, Anthony, 82
Cameron, Charles J., 73
Campbell, Mrs. Patrick, 111, 114, 116
Carew, John, 91
Castlemary, 32
Chapin, Harold, 81
Christians, Mady, 86

154

INDEX

Clarence, O. B., 16, 57
Clements, Frank, 33
Cliffe, H. Cooper, 116
Collier, Constance, 15, 77, 118
Compton, Fay, 2, 11, 26, 69, 77, 118, 153
Cookson, S. A., 8, 37, 73, 142
Copley, Peter, 150
Cottrell, Cherry, 83
Cowie, Laura, 15, 82, 117
Cruickshank, Andrew, 16, 49, 56, 133, 148

DACRE, ARTHUR, 72
Daub, Ellen, 85
David, 32
Davis, " Jew ", 123
Deane, Charles, 57
Decarli, 54
Denis, Frank, 129
de Silva, N., 73, 112, 115
Dessailly, Jean, 39
Devine, George, 82
Devlin, William, 40, 61
Diddear, Charles, 71, 141
Dieglemann, Wilhelm, 38, 99
Dietrich, 117
Dignam, Mark, 150
Dix, Dorothy, 83, 132, 148
Dobson, Owen, 85
Döbbelin, Caroline, 70
Douglas, Marion, 85
Duff, Mary, 2

EASTLAKE, MARY, 62
Ebinger, Blandine, 55
Edwards, Henry, 86
Eggerth, 53
Eibenschütz, Camilla, 75
Eis, Maria, 53
Elliott, Gertrude, 73, 111, 114
Elmy, Mrs., 93, 95

FELICIANI, MARIO, 152
Ffrangcon-Davies, Gwen, 81
Field, Ben, 131
Fitzgerald, Walter, 150
Fleming, Ian, 15, 118
Franca, Celia, 151

GAUGE, ALEXANDER, 65, 87
Genn, Leo, 40
Gerard, Florence, 104
Gish, Lillian, 82
Glen, John, 87
Glenny, Charles, 73, 143
Glover, Julia, 24, 61
Glover, Phillis, 61, 62
Glyn, Isabella, 96
Godfrey, Michael, 87
Goring, Marius, 83
Gough, Michael, 150
Gould, Bernard, 116
Graham, George, 86
Grahame, Ailsa, 87
Grahame, Margot, 103
Granville, Charlotte, 98, 116
Guinness, Alec, 82, 145

HADANK, GÜNTHER, 131
Hamlin, Clement, 86
Hancke, 70, 95
Hanray, Lawrence, 21
Hanson, Valerie, 65
Hardy, Laurence, 153
Hardy, Robert, 153
Hare, Ernest, 40
Harned, Virginia, 112
Harris, Clare, 83, 147
Hart, John, 151
Hawkins, Jack, 2, 26, 40, 41, 82, 131
Heidmann, Manfred, 152
Herlie, Eileen, 103, 149
Hewitt, Muriel, 76
Hobbs, Halliwell, 127
Holloway, Stanley, 135
Holme, Thea, 55
Holmes, Robert, 129, 144
Holt, Maude (Helen Maude, Mrs. Tree), 72, 112, 115
Hordern, Michael, 153
Howe, George, 15, 83
Howe, Henry, 29
Howland, Alan, 76, 129, 144
Howlett, Stanley, 83
Hoyle, James, 56

Hübner, Herbert, 53
Hunt, Martita, 81

IMERSON, A. B., 75
Ishanturayeva, 114

JACKSON, FREDA, 57
Jäger, Hans-Ernst, 152
Jeffries, Douglas, 81
Jones, Owen, 40
Jones, S. Major, 127
Justin, John, 87, 135

KALTHEUNER, WALTER, 152
Karma, 55
Kawakami, Oto, 35
Keen, Malcolm, 15, 43, 77, 81, 82, 118
Kemble, Henry, 72
Kenton, Godfrey, 147
Kidd, John, 87, 148
Kleinoschegg, Willy, 117, 145
Klietch, 54
Knight, Esmond, 8, 135
Knott, Else, 85
Komisarjevskaya, Vera, 111, 114
Komisarov, S. M., 52
Koppenhöfer, Maria, 55, 78
Krausneck, Arthur, 78

LACEY, CATHERINE, 87
Lander, Charles, 143
Lane-Smith, Donald, 83
Lang, 53
Laurier, Jay, 134
Leclercq, Rose, 72
Lefebvre, Rolf, 87
Leigh, Andrew, 83
Leigh, Vivien, 26
Lessen, Kurt, 53
Lessingham, Mrs., 111, 113
Lewes, Miriam, 75
Lindt, 53
Lister, Francis, 135
Locke, Katherine, 86
Lossen, Robert, 152
Lubitsch, Ernst, 128
Lyel, Viola, 86

MACKLIN, F. H., 72
May, Alexander, 152
McNaughton, Gus, 135
Macnee, Patrick, 151
Macready, William Charles, 61
Maitland, Lauderdale, 116
Manning, Henry, 87
Mapp, Neville, 132
March, Ruth, 82
Martin-Harvey, Michael, 86
Massingham, Dorothy, 76, 102, 129, 144
Maude, Helen, see Holt
Mayne, Eric, 107, 116
Mead, Tom, 33
Mestayer, Harry, 82
Michael, Ralph, 81
Milton, Maud, 13, 73, 143
Modjeska, Helena, 111, 113
Morell, André, 133
Morgan, Terence, 118, 149

NALSEN, 54
Napier, Frank, 81
Neilson, Christine, 24
Nemetz, Max, 152
Neville, John, 153
Nevens, Paul, 86
Neville, George, 33
Newton, Robert, 83
Nicholson, H. O., 75

O'BRIEN, TERENCE, 76
Outin, Régis, 39

PAGAY, HANS, 128
Page, Christopher, 87
Paltenghi, David, 151
Paulsen, 54, 117, 145
Pavlov, Muriel, 122
Paxinou, Katina, 49
Ponto, Erich, 54
Price, Dennis, 135
Prior, Mrs., 24

QUARTERMAINE, LÉON, 44
Quayle, Anthony, 8, 16, 87, 133, 148
Quinn, James, 48

RAINFORTH, ELIZABETH, 71
Rawlings, Margaret, 151
Redgrave, Michael, 132, 138
Reibnitz, Ursula von, 152
Reid, David, 86
Relph, George, 77
Rhodes, Percy, 8, 37
Richardson, Ralph, 43
Richter, Walter, 85
Ringham, Walter, 14, 73, 142
Robertson, Ian, 98
Robinson, John, 41
Rodzyalovskaya, 56
Rogers, Paul, 65, 87, 150
Rollett, Raymond, 86
Romano, Colonna, 100
Ross, Frederick, 34, 75
Rotha, Wanda, 150

SANNON, EMILIE, 3
Saunderson, Mary, 93
Scaife, Isobel, 55
Scharwenta, Franz, 53
Schaeffer, Rosel, 152
Schultz, Eva-Katharina, 152
Scott-Gatty, Alex, 14, 142
Scudamore, Margaret, 112
Searle, William, 29, 141
Shakespeare, William, 93
Shaw, Glen Byam, 15, 41, 117, 145
Shaw, Sebastian, 151
Sherry, Craighall, 57
Sherwood, Lydia, 150
Sim, Alastair, 81
Simmons, Jean, 118
Simonov, Rubin, 102
Skillan, George, 83
Skorik, Irene, 138
Soloveyva, V. V., 74
Spencer, Marian, 105, 135
Squire, William, 153
Stagni, Ferruccio, 152
Stewart, Mr., 29
Sullivan, Francis L., 83, 132, 148
Swete, Lyall, 20
Sydney, Basil, 88, 91, 149

TANDY, JESSICA, 82, 117, 118
Tearle, Godfrey, 81
Ternan, Frances, 96
Terry, Ellen, 25, 112, 113
Terry, Kate, 1
Tickle, Frank, 133
Toone, Geoffrey, 21, 145
Tree, Maud, see Holt
Troughton, Patrick, 134
Turleigh, Veronica, 16, 56, 133, 148

VANBRUGH, IRENE, 81
Varden, Norma, 76
Vasilyev, V. I., 52
Vautier, Sydney, 107
Volckmar, 117, 145
Vosper, Frank, 15, 76, 82, 90, 117, 129, 144

WAGNER, FREDA, 53
Waldron, Mr., 71
Warde, James, 29
Waring, Herbert, 15, 77, 81
Warner, Mary (Miss Huddart), 71, 141
Wäscher, 55, 78
Weber, 55
Wegener, Paul, 75, 144
Wenham, Jane, 65, 87
Wenzel, John, 55
Weston, Mrs., *frontispiece*
Widdicombe, Henry, 126
Williams, Harcourt, 34
Williams, Rhys, 86
Wilson, Richard, 67, 70
Winterstein, Eduard von, 38, 128, 144
Woester, Heinz, 145
Wood, George, 83
Woodbridge, George, 135
Wooland, Norman, 8, 147, 149
Wordsworth, Richard, 56
Wright, Cowley, 107
Wright, Fred (Senr.), 73
Wynyard, Diana, 87

YACCO, SADA, 25, 74, 113
Young, Clara Kimble, 3

ZHELINSKY, A. M., 74
Zvezdochotov, 56

PRODUCERS

Akimov, Nicolai, 94, 102, 122, 132, 147
Anderson, J. Grant, 138, 149
Asche, Oscar, 13, 20
Atkins, Robert, 69, 86
Ayliff, H. K., 49, 53, 76, 102, 126, 129, 144

Babakhodjayev, 84, 101
Barker, Will, 3
Barrault, Jean-Louis, 39
Barrett, Wilson, 62
Barrymore, John, 15, 63, 77, 118
Bebutov, Valery, 56
Bel Geddes, Norman, 44
Benson, Frank, 10, 34, 121
Benthall, Michael, 21, 57, 58, 87, 103, 135, 153

Carpenter, Ernest, 25, 34, 107, 116, 127
Chekov, Michael, 77
Coghill, Nevill, 20, 55

Deffontaines, Henri, 3, 100
Dobson, Oliver, 85
Döbbelin, Karl, 67, 70, 95

Edwards, Geoffrey, 88, 91
Edwards, Hilton, 26

Fechter, Charles, 1, 127
Fuchs, George, 6
Furse, Judith, 7, 16, 21, 65, 110, 134

Gade, Svend, 3, 61, 65
Garrick, David, 48, 93
Gassman, Vittorio, 152
Gavelia, Branko, 59
Gielgud, John, 10, 15, 40, 41, 82, 90, 117, 131, 145

Greet, Ben, 25
Gsovsky, Victor, 138
Guinness, Alec, 150
Guthrie, Tyrone, 16, 17, 21, 26, 40, 43, 56, 57, 58, 83, 103, 132, 133, 135, 148

Hagemann, Dr. Carl, 10
Harvey, Martin, 10, 73, 75, 112, 129, 143
Hauptmann, Gerhart, 49, 54, 117, 145
Hauser, Frank, 150
Helpmann, Robert, 24, 151
Hepworth, Cecil, 2, 8, 14, 37
Hilar, Dr. K. H. H., 26, 39
Hopkins, Arthur, 10
Howard, Leslie, 23, 69, 108
Hunt, Hugh, 41, 65, 87, 150

Irving, Henry, 10, 25, 33, 52, 68

Jackson, Barry, 68, 76, 102
Jessner, Leopold, 55, 78, 131

Kawakami, Oto, 25, 35, 74
Kean, Charles, 1, 4, 12, 19, 23, 30, 51, 72, 89, 97, 121, 124, 139, 140
Klein, Caesar, 99, 109
Kvapil, Yaroslav, 80, 103, 110, 130, 146
Komisarjevsky, Th., 111

La Trobe, Charles, 68
Lewinger, Ernst, 6, 143

McClintic, Guthrie, 82
Macready, William Charles, 23, 29, 71, 96, 141
Madjanishvili, 79
Meissner, Hans, 85

Méliès, Georges, 3
Monck, Nugent, 112

Nijinska, Bronislava, 138

O'Farrell, George More, 134, 151
Okhlopkov, Nikolai, 138
Olivier, Laurence, 8, 59, 91, 103, 118, 135, 149

Payne, Iden, 83, 147
Phelps, Samuel, 24, 96
Poel, William, 112, 115
Prentice, Herbert, 68

Reinhardt, Max, 25, 38, 68, 75, 99, 128, 144
Röbbeling, 53
Robertson, Forbes, 10, 73, 81, 98, 116, 142
Rylands, George, 42, 84, 105, 135

Saxe-Meiningen, Duke of, 121
Schalla, Hans, 94, 152
Schröder, Friedrich, 67
Southern, E. H., 112
Stanislavsky, Constantin, 25, 36, 52, 74
Stejskal, Bohus, 68
Szyffman, Arnold, 42, 54, 91, 101

Tearle, Godfrey, 69
Tree, Beerbohm, 72

Uigur, M., 84, 101

Wangenheim, Gustav V., 49
Webster, Margaret, 86
Williams, Harcourt, 10, 43, 81
Wolfit, Donald, 138

Young, James, 3

DESIGNERS

Akimov, Nicolai, 102, 132, 147
Andreu, Mariano, 150
Appia, Adolf, 25
Ayrton, Randle, 83, 147

Bailey, James, 87, 135
Barlow, Alan, 65, 87
Battersby, Martin, 40, 132, 148
Bax, Peter, 134, 151
Bel Geddes, Norman, 44
Beverley, William, 96
Bragdon, Claude, 7, 64, 100
Broadfoot, W., 126
Buckle, Richard, 20, 55
Burnand, John, 91

Carrick, Edward, 61
Chaney, Stewart, 108
Chaperon, 32
Chiari, Mario, 152
Cochrane, Jeanetta, 105, 135
Craig, E. Gordon, 2, 25, 36, 52, 61, 68, 74
Craven, Hawes, 33, 52, 68, 116, 142
Curtis, Barbara, 83, 147
Cuthbert, H., 4, 19, 72, 89, 124

Day, I., 97
Dodson, George J., 73, 143

Erler, Fritz, 2, 6

Fenton, 96
ffolkes, David, 86
Finlay, 96
Fritzsche, Max, 94, 152
Frycz, Karol, 42, 55, 91, 101, 128
Furse, Roger, 8, 16, 43, 56, 57, 58, 59, 91, 103, 118, 133, 135, 148, 149

Gade, Svend, 108, 109, 126
Gates, James, 126

Godwin, E. W., 61, 62
Grieve, Thomas, 1, 4, 12, 19, 23, 30, 31, 51, 72, 89, 97, 124, 139, 140

Hagemann, Dr. Carl, 10, 14, 35, 98, 127
Hammond, Aubrey, 81
Hann, Walter, 92
Harker, Joseph, 13, 20
Harris, Margaret, 40
Harvey, Martin, 75, 129
Heltzer, 5
Heslewood, Tom, 13, 20
Hofman, Vlastial, 26, 39, 79, 90, 130, 146
Hurry, Leslie, 21, 57, 58, 103, 135, 151

Irving, Laurence, 41, 150
Israel, 121

Jakameit, Rosemarie, 138
Jaschimovicz, T., 121, 125
Jones, 12, 30, 51, 139, 140
Jones, Robert Edmond, 15, 63, 77, 118

Karl, 72, 73, 98, 116, 142
Keating, Ruth, 105, 135
Kilian, Eugen, 99, 109

Lechner, 30
Lefler, Professor, 126
Libakov, M. V., 77
Libermann, 121
Linnebach, Adolf, 2
Littman, Max, 2

Macquoid, Percy, 81
Mahnke, Adolf, 54, 117, 145
Masson, André, 39
Meiklejohn, Maisie, 65

Mielziner, Jo, 82
Motley, 10, 15, 40, 41, 82, 90, 117, 131, 145

Neher, Caspar, 55, 78, 85, 131
Neville, Mr., 126
Nicholls, E. C., 34, 107, 116, 127
Nicholls, Mr., 96

Robinson, Osborne, 40, 83, 132, 148
Rowell, Kenneth, 153
Rube, 32
Ryndin, V., 138

Sanquirico, Alessandro, 32
Schumacher, Fritz, 6, 143
Sebree, Charles, 85
Shelving, Paul, 49, 52, 76, 102, 126, 129, 144
Sheppard, Guy, 86
Shlepyanov, I. Y., 84, 101
Smyth, Owen P., 43, 81
Solomons, Gladstone, 149
Stern, Ernst, 38, 75, 99, 128, 144
Strnad, Oskar, 64
Sulerzhitsky, L. A., 36

Telbin, William (Snr.), 1, 5, 13, 31, 97, 125
Telbin, William (Jnr.), 72
Treeck, Therese van, 152
Troster, Frantisek, 68

Varga, M., 63

Warre, Michael, 7, 16, 21, 65, 110, 134
Wenig, Josef, 80, 103, 110, 130, 146
Wright, Geoffrey, 42, 84
Wijdeveld, H. th., 38, 89

Zedrinski, V., 59

INDEX

COUNTRIES AND THEATRES

ARGENTINA
   BUENOS AYRES
      Colon, 138

AUSTRIA
   VIENNA, 25, 49, 67, 68
      Burgtheater, 64
      Carltheater, 121
      Deutsches Volkstheater, 53, 126
      Josefstheater, 121
      Opera House, 121

BELGIUM
   BRUSSELS, 11

CANADA, 138

CHINA, 25

CZECHOSLOVAKIA, 26
   PRAGUE
      Hibernian, 26
      Municipal, 68, 80, 103, 110, 130, 146,
      National, 26, 39, 49, 68, 79, 90, 130, 146
      V. Kotcich, 26

DENMARK
   ELSINORE
      Kronborg Castle, 11, 26, 40, 41, 61, 69, 138, 153

ENGLAND
   BATH
      Theatre Royal, 23, 28, 67
   BIRMINGHAM
      Repertory, 68
   BRISTOL
      Theatre Royal, 61, 65, 87
   BROMLEY
      New Theatre, 88, 91
   CAMBRIDGE
      The Arts (Marlowe Society), 26, 42, 84
   LONDON
      Adelphi, 13, 20, 52
      Arts Theatre Club, 2, 7, 16, 21, 24, 65, 110, 112, 134
      Carpenters' Hall, 112
      City of London, 24
      Court, 11
      Covent Garden, 1, 23, 29, 48, 50, 51, 62, 67, 68, 71, 75, 96, 121, 122
      Curtain, 112
      Drury Lane, *frontispiece*, 1, 2, 24, 27, 28, 29, 48, 49, 50, 52, 67, 68, 70, 73, 93, 95, 113, 121, 123, 142
      Globe (Bankside), 93, 112
      Globe (Old), 25
      Haymarket, 10, 15, 23, 27, 29, 50, 51, 62, 63, 67, 68, 72, 77, 81, 93, 96, 105, 118, 123, 129, 135, 138, 141
      Her Majesty's, 67, 68
      Imperial, 24
      Kingsway, 11, 49, 68, 76, 102, 129, 138, 144
      Lincoln's Inn, 93
      Lyceum, 1, 5, 10, 11, 13, 24, 25, 31, 33, 34, 52, 68, 97, 98, 107, 111, 113, 114, 116, 125, 127
      Lyric, 68, 73, 114, 115, 143
      Marylebone, 24
      New, 10, 11, 15, 21, 26, 40, 57, 58, 82, 90, 103, 117, 118, 131, 135, 145, 150, 151

ENGLAND
   LONDON
      New Boltons, 49
      New Oxford, 11, 112
      Old Vic, 10, 11, 16, 17, 18, 26, 43, 56, 57, 58, 69, 81, 83, 93, 112, 132, 133, 138, 148
      Olympic, 25
      Pavilion (Mile End Road), 24
      Princess's, 1, 2, 4, 12, 19, 30, 51, 62, 72, 89, 94, 96, 97, 126, 139, 140
      Queen's, 10
      Rudolph Steiner Hall, 112
      Sadler's Wells, 24, 33, 93, 96
      St. James's, 61
      Standard (Shoreditch), 24
      Surrey, 24, 33
      The Theatre, 112
      Westminster, 26
   MANCHESTER
      Theatre Royal, 25, 121
   NORWICH
      Maddermarket, 112
   OXFORD
      New, 20, 55
      Playhouse, 112
      University Dramatic Society (O.U.D.S.), 17, 20, 26, 55, 112
   STRATFORD-UPON-AVON
      Memorial, 11, 18, 25, 49, 69, 83, 86, 87, 135, 138, 147
   WINDSOR
      Windsor Castle, 23, 31
   YORK
      Theatre Royal, 24

FINLAND
   HELSINGFORS
      Svenska, 26

FRANCE
   PARIS
      Comédie Française, 49
      Marigny, 39
      Opera House, 24, 32
      Théâtre Français, 49

GERMANY, 25
   BERLIN, 67, 68, 70, 95
      Court, 30
      Deutsches Theater, 38, 49, 75, 99, 128, 144
      Neues Schauspielhaus, 109, 126
      State, 26, 55, 65, 78, 131
   BOCHUM
      Park Theatre, 94
   DRESDEN
      Court, 6, 143
      State Theatre, 49, 54, 117, 145
   FRANKFURT
      Frankfurt Festival, 69, 85
   HAMBURG, 6
      Thaliatheater, 53
   MANNHEIM
      Court, 10, 14, 35, 98, 127
   MUNICH, 138
      Court, 99, 109
      Künstler, 2, 6

HOLLAND
   AMSTERDAM
      Municipal, 38, 89

HUNGARY
   BUDAPEST
      National, 63

INDIA, 138
   BOMBAY
      Opera House, 149

IRELAND
   DUBLIN
      Gate, 26
      Theatre Royal, 123
   KILKENNY
      Theatre Royal, 24

ITALY
   MILAN
      La Scala, 23, 32
   NAPLES
      San Carlo, 138
   ROME
      Teatro Valle, 152

JAPAN, 25
   TOKIO, 35, 74, 113

NORWAY
   OSLO
      National, 26

POLAND
   WARSAW
      Imperial, 113
      Polski, 42, 54, 91, 128

RUSSIA (U.S.S.R.)
   MOSCOW
      Art, 25, 36, 52, 74, 77
      Mayakousky, 138
      Vakhtangov, 102, 132, 147
   PETROGRAD
      Imperial Alexandriisky, 5, 111, 114
   BELORUSSIA : VITEBSK
      State Dramatic, 56
   GEORGIA : TBILISI
      Rustavelli, 68, 79
   UZBEKISTAN : TASHKENT
      Uzbek State, 69, 84, 114

SCOTLAND
   EDINBURGH
      Theatre Royal, 48, 61
      Edinburgh Festival, 26, 49, 61
   ABERDEEN, 61

SOUTH AFRICA, 138

SWEDEN, 121
   STOCKHOLM
      National, 126
   NORKOPINE-LINKORING
      State, 26

UNITED STATES OF AMERICA, 25
   NEW YORK, 1, 2, 10, 24, 61, 68, 69, 88, 111, 121, 138
      Bowery, 2
      Broadhurst, 44
      Empire, 82
      Hampden's, 7, 64
      Hampton Institute, 85
      New Theatre, Chappel Street, 2
      St. James's, 86
   PENNSYLVANIA, 2
   PHILADELPHIA, 2
   VIRGINIA
      State, 26

YUGOSLAVIA
   LJUBLJANA
      National, 59

INDEX

MISCELLANEOUS

ARTISTS AND ENGRAVERS

Clint, George, 62
Cruikshank, George, 27, 121

Daniels, Wm., 104
De Wilde, Samuel, 122
Dighton, Robert, 62
Dunkerton, Robert, 96

Hamilton, Mary, 123
Hayman, Francis, 93, 95

McArdell, J., 23
Mortimer, 28

Roberts, James, 95

Scharf, Sir George, (*Scenic Recollections of Covent Garden Theatre, 1838–9*), 23

Walker, 28
Wilson, Benjamin, 23

Zoffany, John, 50

BOOKS: GENERAL

Art of the Theatre (Gordon Craig), 2, 25
Art of the Theatre (Carl Hagemann), 10

Complete History of Theatrical Entertainments at the English Court (Ed. J. K. Chapman), 23

Letters and Poems of John Henderson (John Ireland), 93
Life and Enterprises of R. W. Elliston (George Raymond), 27

Memoirs of Grimaldi ("Boz" — Charles Dickens), 121
Music and Stage Setting (Adolf Appia), 25

Revolution of the Theatre (George Fuchs), 2

Towards a New Theatre (Gordon Craig), 25

COLLECTIONS

British Museum, 123

Garrick Club, 48, 95

Maugham, W. Somerset (National Theatre Collection), 70

National Portrait Gallery, 96
Niessen, Dr. Carl, 23

Victoria and Albert Museum, 1, 62, 104
Vienna State Library, 112

COMPOSERS

Blacher, Boris, 24, 138
Honegger, Arthur, 26
Liszt, Franz, 24

Tchaikovsky, 24, 138, 151
Thomas, Ambroise, 24, 32

Walton, Sir William, 3

BALLETS

La Nijinska Company, Paris, 138

Munich Company, 138

Sadler's Wells Company, 138, 151
San Carlo, Naples, 138

COSTUME

Hamlet (Character), 1, 23, 48–9, 61, 93, 104, 123

Modern Dress Productions: 11, 16, 25, 35, 43, 49, 53, 55, 56, 57, 58, 68, 69, 74, 76, 78, 80, 87, 88, 102, 103, 110, 113, 126, 129, 130, 131, 133, 138, 144, 146, 148

Ophelia, 94, 111, 122

EDITIONS AND VERSIONS

Dog Hamlets, 24

Folio and Quartos, 112
Fratricide Punished, or Hamlet Prince of Denmark, 112

G.I. Hamlet, 69
Grave Burst, or The Ghost's Piteous Tale of Horror, 2

Hanner, Sir Thos. (Ed.), 93

Illustrated Editions, 93

Kyd, Thomas, 112

Nazi Hamlet, 61, 65
Nicholas Rowe (Ed.), Jacob Tonson (Publisher), 93, 95

Princess Hamlet (Danish Legend), 61

Theobald (Ed.), Jacob Tonson (Publisher), 93, 95

Wilson, Dover, 11

FILMS

Versions of Hamlet, 2, 3, 8, 14, 37, 59, 61, 65, 68, 91, 100, 103, 105, 118, 135, 149

GRAMOPHONE RECORDS

Excerpts from Hamlet, 3

OPERAS

Mercadanti, 23, 32

Thomas, Ambroise, 24, 32

RECORD RUNS

London and New York, 2

STAGE EFFECTS

Pepper's Ghost, 1

Trap Door, 27

TELEVISION

B.B.C., 69, 122, 134, 151

JUVENILE DRAMA AND MODEL THEATRE (Publishers)

Hodgson, 67, 71, 141

Jameson, 3

Trensensky, 121, 125

West, 1, 3, 4, 12, 19, 105, 107, 124, 139, 140

SOCIETIES

Elizabethan Stage Society, 112

Fellowship of Players, 69

Shakespeare Reading Society, 112

TRANSLATORS, LIBRETTISTS, ADAPTERS, ETC.

Barbier, 24

Caré, 24
Cankar, Ivan, 26

Dent, Alan, 3
Dukis, Jean-Louis, 49

Eschenburg, Johann, 94

German, Edward, 24
Gide, André, 26, 49

Hayes, Dan, 24

Kolar, J. J., 68

Romani, 23

Saudek, Erik, 68
Schlegel, A. W., 49
Scoumel, 68
Sladek, 26, 68
Squarzina, Luigi, 138
Stepanek, B., 26

ST. MARY'S COLLEGE OF MARYLAND
ST. MARY'S CITY, MARYLAND

053769